A GUIDE TO

TITUS ANDRONICUS

The Shakespeare Handbooks

Guides currently available:

- Antony and Cleopatra
- As You Like It
- The Comedy of Errors
- Coriolanus
- Cymbeline
- Hamlet
- Henry IV, Part 1
- Henry IV, Part 2
- Henry V
- Julius Caesar
- King Lear
- Love's Labour's Lost
- Macbeth
- Measure for Measure
- The Merchant of Venice
- The Merry Wives of Windsor
- A Midsummer Night's Dream
- Much Ado About Nothing
- Othello
- Pericles
- Richard II
- Richard III
- Romeo and Juliet
- The Tempest
- Titus Andronicus
- Twelfth Night
- The Winter's Tale

A Guide to
Titus Andronicus

by Alistair McCallum

Upstart Crow Publications

First published in 2025 by
Upstart Crow Publications

Copyright © Alistair McCallum 2025

A CIP catalogue record for this book
is available from the British Library

ISBN 978 1 899747 27 6

www.shakespeare-handbooks.com

Setting the scene

Shakespeare probably wrote *Titus Andronicus* in 1592–3, when he was in his late twenties. The first recorded performance of the play was in 1594; unusually, it was also produced as a printed booklet (a 'quarto') in the same year, suggesting it was popular with both audiences and readers.

Few details of Shakespeare's early career are known, but he had probably arrived in London in the late 1580s intending to establish himself as an actor. Although he undoubtedly had some success, and continued acting for many years, he appears to have turned his attention to writing soon after arriving in the capital, and he quickly made a name for himself as both a poet and a playwright. His earliest plays included histories and comedies; *Titus Andronicus* was his first venture into tragedy, and its success confirmed his reputation as one of England's leading writers. A few months after the play's first performances, the thirty-year-old Shakespeare became a member of a theatre company that would prove immensely successful over the next two decades.

Titus Andronicus explores themes of justice, crime and vengeance, and is notorious for its relentless brutality, both offstage and onstage. Such 'revenge plays' were hugely popular in Elizabethan England, just as horror films are today; however, the genre fell out of favour towards the end of the 17th century as theatrical tastes became more refined. Critics and scholars generally considered the play primitive and barbaric, and many insisted that it could not have been written by Shakespeare. As a result, the play virtually disappeared from view for over two hundred years.

The second half of the 20th century saw renewed interest in the play, and although it remains a challenging experience for modern audiences it is, in the 21st century, becoming an established part of the theatrical landscape:

"It is little wonder, in a century where nihilism and the absurd have been key artistic and philosophical responses to unspeakable horrors of the world, that Titus Andronicus *has re-found its place as one of Shakespeare's most relevant and prescient works."*

Karin Brown, *Titus Andronicus in Performance*, in the RSC Shakespeare edition of *Titus Andronicus*, 2011

An important decision

The Roman emperor has died, and Rome is in mourning. A new emperor must now be chosen: both the wealthy, aristocratic senators of Rome and the tribunes, representing the Roman people, will have a say in the election of a successor.

The two sons of the late emperor are candidates for election, the older son being the customary choice. However, candidates from outside the imperial family or the world of politics may also be chosen. Military leaders, especially those who have conquered new lands for Rome, are particularly popular with the citizens. One such leader is the general Titus Andronicus: he has just defeated the Goths, Rome's old enemy on the empire's northern frontier, a people regarded by the Romans as troublesome and barbarous.

The choice of a successor will be made in the Capitol, the political heart of Rome. Although in mourning, the area is bustling with activity as senators and tribunes discuss the urgent matter of selecting the next emperor.

Curtain up

A question of succession

The Roman emperor has died, and the mood in the Capitol, the empire's seat of government, is solemn. The tribunes, representatives of the Roman people, have gathered there, along with the senators, Rome's aristocratic lawmakers.

Just outside the Capitol, however, the atmosphere of solemnity has been disrupted by a confrontation which threatens to erupt into outright violence. The emperor's two sons, Saturninus and Bassianus, each accompanied by an armed gang of supporters, are facing up to one another defiantly. Saturninus, the older son, claims that the title of emperor is now his by right and tradition. He calls out to those around him, and to the senators in the Capitol, to support him with force if necessary:

Saturninus: Noble patricians,[1] patrons[2] of my right,
Defend the justice of my cause with arms;
And countrymen, my loving followers,
Plead my successive title[3] with your swords.

[1] *aristocrats*
[2] *protectors, guardians*
[3] *support my right to succeed as emperor*

"The first scene reveals the play's central question: what principles should govern a good society? This problem is presented in the conflict between Saturninus and Bassianus, sons of the deceased emperor and rivals for the imperial crown. As the eldest, Saturninus' claim is based on tradition, custom and primogeniture. He pleads with the citizens of Rome to honor his 'right', and defend his 'successive title' with their swords. However, the claim of the younger son, Bassianus, is based on personal worth and virtue; his appeal is to justice, honor and freedom of choice. Such a split between rights and merits at the highest level suggests a fundamental fracture in the veneer of Roman society, and projects a sense of the slippery nature of justice itself."

Judith Bock, *A Wilderness of Tigers*, 1988

Bassianus insists that he is a far more suitable candidate for the title of emperor than his brother, who is known, he claims, to be a corrupt and immoral individual:

Bassianus: … suffer not dishonour to approach
The imperial seat, to virtue consecrate,
To justice, continence and nobility; [1]
But let desert in pure election shine, [2]
And, Romans, fight for freedom in your choice.

[1] *do not allow the position of emperor, which should
be dedicated to virtue, justice, self-control and
nobility, to be tainted by dishonour*
[2] *through your free choice, let the worthier candidate
succeed*

The atmosphere grows more and more menacing; but before the dispute can escalate any further, a commanding voice silences the brothers and their supporters. The speaker is Marcus Andronicus, chief Tribune of the People, who has emerged from the Capitol to address the crowd. In his hands is the crown which will be presented to the new emperor.

The citizens of Rome have made their choice, announces Marcus. Ignoring the claims of the late emperor's two sons, the people have nominated Marcus's brother Titus, a highly respected Roman general, as the next emperor:

Marcus: Princes, that strive by factions and by friends
Ambitiously for rule and empery, [1]
Know that the people of Rome, for whom we stand
A special party, [2] have by common voice
In election for the Roman empery
Chosen Andronicus, surnamed Pius [3]
For many good and great deserts [4] to Rome.
A nobler man, a braver warrior,
Lives not this day within the city walls.

[1] *who are struggling, along with your friends and
supporters, to achieve the status of emperor*
[2] *whose interests we, the tribunes, represent*
[3] *given the honorary name Pius, meaning devout,
dutiful and just*
[4] *deeds worthy of reward*

For the last ten years, Titus has been fighting a long, exhausting campaign against the Goths, Rome's enemy in the north. The war has been arduous and bloody, and Titus has lost several of his sons in the conflict: finally, however, the Goths have been defeated, and Titus is about to return victorious to Rome.

As representative of the Roman people, Marcus intends to propose Titus Andronicus as the next emperor. Saturninus and Bassianus are free to present themselves to the senate as candidates, he declares, but only if they dismiss their armed followers. The brothers willingly do so, and peace descends as the crowd disperses. The two young men follow Marcus as he returns to the Capitol.

An eye for an eye

The calm outside the Capitol is short-lived. The silence is shattered as a large military procession approaches, heralded by the warlike sound of drums and trumpets: the conquering army of Titus Andronicus has returned from the wars.

First in the procession are Titus's four sons, followed by Titus himself. A group of captives is then revealed, including the Queen of the Goths along with her sons and followers. The mood is not purely triumphant, however: in the midst of the procession are two coffins, draped in black cloth, containing the bodies of two of Titus's sons, killed in the fierce fighting against the Goths.

Titus is overcome with emotion as he sets foot in his home city after his long absence. Just as he is grieving for his dead sons, the city is mourning the death of the emperor:

> *Titus:*   Hail, Rome, victorious in thy mourning weeds! [1]
> Lo, as the bark that hath discharged his freight
> Returns with precious lading to the bay
> From whence at first she weighed her anchorage, [2]
> Cometh Andronicus, bound with laurel boughs, [3]
> To resalute his country with his tears …

> [1] *garments, attire*
> [2] *like a ship that has discharged its original cargo and returned home carrying precious merchandise*
> [3] *wearing the symbol of victory*

His first task, Titus announces, will be to bury his two sons, the latest of many to die in battle. He appeals to the god Jupiter, protector of Rome, to look upon him favourably as he carries out the funeral rites.

The tomb of the Andronicus family is nearby. The vault is opened, and Titus reflects sadly on the sons he has lost as he contemplates the bodies within. Lucius, his oldest surviving son, calls for the death of one of their captives, to pacify the spirits of the dead warriors and to prevent the appearance of evil omens in the future:

Titus:	O sacred receptacle of my joys,
	Sweet cell of virtue and nobility,
	How many sons hast thou of mine in store
	That thou wilt never render to me more! [1]
Lucius:	Give us the proudest prisoner of the Goths,
	That we may hew his limbs and on a pile
	Ad manes fratrum [2] sacrifice his flesh
	Before this earthly prison of their bones, [3]
	That so the shadows be not unappeased,
	Nor we disturbed with prodigies on earth. [4]

[1] *that you, the tomb, will never give back to me*
[2] *to our brothers' spirits*
[3] *in front of their grave*
[4] *so that their ghosts will be satisfied, and we will not be troubled by unnatural events here on earth*

Titus agrees, and to the horror of Tamora, the Queen of the Goths, he singles out her eldest son Alarbus. She kneels before Titus, begging him to change his mind. Her love for her son is every bit as strong as Titus's for his own sons:

Tamora:	[*kneeling*] Stay,[1] Roman brethren! Gracious conqueror,
	Victorious Titus, rue [2] the tears I shed,
	A mother's tears in passion for her son.
	And if thy sons were ever dear to thee,
	O, think my son to be as dear to me!

[1] *stop, wait*
[2] *have pity on*

Her son is guilty only of fighting for his nation, which Titus must surely regard as a noble activity, pleads Tamora: besides, a leader of his stature should favour mercy, not vengeance. Titus remains firm. He is sympathetic with the queen, even apologetic; but he insists that the young man's death is a religious necessity.

Lucius and his brothers drag Alarbus away, keen to hack up his body and see it devoured by fire. This is barbarity, Tamora declares bitterly, and has nothing to do with religious observance:

Lucius: Away with him, and make a fire straight,[1]
             And with our swords upon a pile of wood
             Let's hew his limbs till they be clean consumed.
             [*Titus's sons leave with Alarbus*]
Tamora: [*rising from her knees*] O cruel, irreligious piety!

[1] *immediately*

Tamora turns to her other sons, Demetrius and Chiron, who, like her, are appalled at the Romans' conduct. Speaking aside, Demetrius assures her that she will have her revenge.

A few minutes later, Lucius and his brothers return. The sacrifice has been made, Lucius announces proudly:

Lucius: See, lord and father, how we have performed
             Our Roman rites: Alarbus' limbs are lopped
             And entrails feed the sacrificing fire,
             Whose smoke like incense doth perfume the sky.

"This woman, a queen, a warrior, now conquered and captive, in an instant perceives where true barbarity lies ... Tamora as prisoner has no recourse to justice, but she will teach Titus a lesson, the brutal lesson of revenge. And we don't blame her; in fact, we take her part. We sympathetically become Goth, and for a time prey on this self-righteous and murderous family that cannot bury its own dead without adding another body to the pile."

Dr Susan Willis, *Shakespeare's Double Helix*, 2007

It is time for Titus to lay his two dead sons to rest. As their coffins are placed in the family tomb, military trumpets are sounded, and Titus says his final farewell. His only consolation is that the troubles of this world can no longer harm them:

Titus:
In peace and honour rest you here, my sons;
Rome's readiest champions,[1] repose you here in rest,
Secure from worldly chances[2] and mishaps.
Here lurks no treason, here no envy[3] swells,
Here grow no damned drugs,[4] here are no storms,
No noise, but silence and eternal sleep:
In peace and honour rest you here, my sons.

[1] most eager defenders
[2] accidents, misfortunes
[3] malice
[4] poisonous weeds

A new emperor is chosen

Titus's daughter Lavinia now appears. She greets her father lovingly, tearful both through sorrow at her brothers' death and with joy at her father's return after his long absence. Titus is delighted to be reunited with his only daughter, and his greeting is warm and heartfelt:

Lavinia:
Lo, at this tomb my tributary tears
I render for my brethren's obsequies,[1]
[kneeling] And at thy feet I kneel with tears of joy
Shed on this earth for thy return to Rome.
O bless me here with thy victorious hand,
Whose fortunes Rome's best citizens applaud.
Titus:
Kind Rome, that hast thus lovingly reserved[2]
The cordial[3] of mine age to glad my heart.
Lavinia live, outlive thy father's days
And fame's eternal date, for virtue's praise.[4]

[1] I shed these tears in tribute to my brothers'
    funeral rites
[2] preserved, protected
[3] comforting medicine
[4] may your goodness allow you to live longer than
    your father, and longer even than fame itself

Marcus Andronicus, Tribune of the People, emerges from the Capitol to welcome his brother Titus back to Rome. Marcus is carrying a pure white robe, the traditional Roman garment of those seeking high political office. The people of Rome want Titus as their emperor, Marcus reveals, and he asks his brother to present himself as a candidate, along with the late emperor's sons, to the Senate:

Marcus: Titus Andronicus, the people of Rome,
Whose friend in justice thou hast ever been,
Send thee by me, their tribune and their trust,
This palliament[1] of white and spotless hue,
And name thee in election for the empire[2]
With these our late-deceased emperor's sons.
Be *candidatus*[3] then, and put it on,
And help to set a head on headless Rome.

[1] *robe, cloak*
[2] *nominate you as a candidate for emperor*
[3] *(Latin) clothed in white*

Titus is taken aback at this unexpected proposal. He makes it clear at once that he would not be a suitable candidate; he is too old, he claims, and in all probability it would not be long before the process of choosing a new emperor would have to start all over again. Besides, although he welcomes the respect of the Roman people, he is not interested in political power:

Titus: A better head her glorious body fits[1]
Than his that shakes for age and feebleness.
What[2] should I don this robe and trouble you?
… Give me a staff of honour for mine age,
But not a sceptre to control the world.

[1] *Rome deserves a better head*
[2] *why*

Marcus persists, confident that Titus will be chosen as emperor if he puts himself forward. However, the other two candidates, the late emperor's sons Saturninus and Bassianus, are nearby, and they overhear the conversation. Saturninus, more impetuous than his younger brother, responds furiously. He believes the position is his by right, and suspects that Marcus is trying to gain power for his own family:

Marcus:	Titus, thou shalt obtain and ask the empery.[1]
Saturninus:	Proud and ambitious tribune, canst thou tell?[2]
Titus:	Patience, prince Saturninus.
Saturninus:	Romans, do me right.
	Patricians, draw your swords, and sheathe them not
	Till Saturninus be Rome's emperor.

> [1] *you need only ask, and the title of emperor will be yours*
> [2] *how do you know?*

Titus eventually calms Saturninus down, assuring the young man that he himself has no interest in becoming emperor. Bassianus, Saturninus's brother and rival, now addresses Titus, appealing humbly for his support. However, Titus has made his decision. Once he has established that he has the backing of the assembled politicians, he asks whether they will accept the candidate that he chooses. They agree willingly, and he states that, in accordance with tradition, the emperor's crown should go to Saturninus:

Titus:	People of Rome, and people's tribunes here,
	I ask your voices and your suffrages:[1]
	Will ye bestow them friendly on Andronicus?
Tribunes:	To gratify the good Andronicus
	And gratulate[2] his safe return to Rome,
	The people will accept whom he admits.[3]
Titus:	Tribunes, I thank you, and this suit[4] I make,
	That you create[5] our emperor's eldest son,
	Lord Saturnine, whose virtues will, I hope,
	Reflect on Rome as Titan's[6] rays on earth ...
	Then if you will elect by my advice,
	Crown him and say, 'Long live our emperor!'

[1] *support and votes*
[2] *celebrate*
[3] *whoever he recognises as emperor*
[4] *request*
[5] *appoint, select*
[6] *the sun-god*

Bright prospects

Rome has a new emperor, and the scene outside the Capitol is one of noisy celebration as the cheering of tribunes, senators, soldiers and citizens is mingled with the beating of drums and the blare of trumpets.

Saturninus, gratified that he has achieved his ambition and inherited his father's crown, turns to Titus. He deserves to be richly rewarded, Saturninus tells him, and as part of that reward his daughter Lavinia will be made Empress of Rome:

> *Saturninus:* Titus Andronicus, for thy favours done
> To us in our election this day,
> I give thee thanks in part of thy deserts,
> And will with deeds requite thy gentleness; [1]
> And for an onset, [2] Titus, to advance
> Thy name and honourable family,
> Lavinia will I make my empress,
> Rome's royal mistress …
>
> [1] *as a partial reward, I now offer you my thanks,*
>   *and my future actions will fully repay your nobility*
> [2] *start, first step*

Saturninus intends to marry Lavinia in the Pantheon, Rome's most magnificent temple. Titus is delighted at the prospect, and in recognition of the honour of becoming the emperor's father-in-law he presents his weapons, his chariot and the spoils of war – including his prisoners – to Saturninus.

Titus now turns to Tamora, the captured queen of the Goths, and assures her that the emperor will treat her kindly. Saturninus confirms that he will indeed show the queen the respect that she deserves. He comments appreciatively on her beauty:

> *Saturninus:* A goodly lady, trust me, of the hue [1]
> That I would choose, were I to choose anew.
> Clear up, fair queen, that cloudy countenance:
> Though chance of war hath wrought this change of
>   cheer, [2]
> Thou com'st not to be made a scorn [3] in Rome.
> Princely shall be thy usage [4] every way.

Rest on my word, and let not discontent
Daunt all your hopes.

[1] *complexion, appearance*
[2] *the misfortunes of war have made you unhappy*
[3] *mocked, abused*
[4] *treatment*

Saturninus, aware that he is paying Tamora undue attention, asks Lavinia whether she is offended; she replies graciously that such courtesy befits an emperor. Pleased with her response, Saturninus declares that all the captives are to be released immediately:

Saturninus:	Lavinia, you are not displeased with this?
Lavinia:	Not I, my lord, sith[1] true nobility
	Warrants these words in princely courtesy.
Saturninus:	Thanks, sweet Lavinia. Romans, let us go.
	Ransomless[2] here we set our prisoners free.
	Proclaim our honours, lords, with trump[3] and drum.

[1] *since*
[2] *without demanding payment from the enemy;*
   unconditionally
[3] *trumpets*

With a fanfare and noisy celebrations, the prisoners are unchained. Among them are Tamora, the queen; her two sons, Chiron and Demetrius; and her African attendant Aaron.

A fatal blow

Saturninus and his attendants are about to leave. A sudden commotion arises, however, when his younger brother Bassianus takes hold of Lavinia. It now becomes clear that Titus's daughter was already engaged to Bassianus, and the young man refuses to allow her marriage to the emperor:

Bassianus:	Lord Titus, by your leave, this maid is mine.
	[*he seizes Lavinia*]
Titus:	How, sir? Are you in earnest then, my lord?
Bassianus:	Ay, noble Titus, and resolved withal
	To do myself this reason and this right.[1]

[1] *to take this reasonable and just action*

Titus's brother Marcus and his son Lucius both agree that, as the two of them are betrothed, Bassianus is justified in asserting his right to marry Lavinia. Titus is furious: he has promised the emperor his daughter's hand in marriage, and it is unthinkable that he should break his word.

Two of Titus's sons help Bassianus to escape with Lavinia. Titus calls out for assistance as he sets out after them. Another of his sons, Mutius, however, stands in Titus's way and refuses to let him pass. Titus, enraged, strikes the young man with such violence that he dies instantly.

Lucius is horrified at his father's brutality. Titus, unrepentant, denounces his sons as traitors, and demands Lavinia's return. Lucius, equally determined, states that she will never marry Saturninus, come what may:

Lucius:	My lord, you are unjust, and more than so;
	In wrongful quarrel you have slain your son.
Titus:	Nor thou, nor he, are any sons of mine;
	My sons would never so dishonour me.
	Traitor, restore Lavinia to the emperor.
Lucius:	Dead if you will, but not to be his wife
	That is another's lawful promised love.[1]

[1] *she will never return to him alive, and will never marry anyone other than her beloved Bassianus, to whom she is engaged*

Rejection

Saturninus, humiliated by the departure of Lavinia, addresses Titus sternly. His tone is bitter and resentful as he tells the ageing general that he and his family are no longer welcome in the emperor's company. Titus is horrified:

Saturninus: No, Titus, no, the emperor needs her[1] not;
Nor her, nor thee, nor any of thy stock.[2]
I'll trust by leisure[3] him that mocks me once;
Thee never, nor thy traitorous haughty sons,
Confederates all[4] thus to dishonour me …
Titus: O monstrous! What reproachful words are these?

[1] *Lavinia*
[2] *family*
[3] *I'm reluctant to trust*
[4] *who have all conspired together*

The emperor dismisses Titus contemptuously. His daughter is worthless, he tells him, and his sons are common ruffians. His own brother Bassianus is no better:

Saturninus: But go thy ways,[1] go give that changing piece[2]
To him that flourished for her with his sword.[3]
A valiant son-in-law thou shalt enjoy,
One fit to bandy[4] with thy lawless sons,
To ruffle[5] in the commonwealth of Rome.
Titus: These words are razors to my wounded heart.

[1] *go away, get out of my sight*
[2] *worthless, fickle woman*
[3] *to Bassianus, who ostentatiously brandished his sword for her*
[4] *brawl*
[5] *create a disturbance*

Saturninus now makes a sudden, unexpected announcement. He turns to the foreign queen who, as Titus's prisoner, caught his eye just a few minutes ago:

Saturninus: And therefore, lovely Tamora, queen of Goths,
That like the stately Phoebe 'mongst her nymphs
Dost overshine the gallant'st dames of Rome,[1]
If thou be pleased with this my sudden choice,
Behold, I choose thee, Tamora, for my bride,
And will create thee empress of Rome.

[1] *who surpasses the finest women in Rome, just as the goddess of the moon outshines her attendant spirits*

They should make their way to the Pantheon, declares the emperor, and marry without delay. Tamora is happy to accept his proposal:

Tamora: … here in sight of heaven to Rome I swear,
If Saturnine advance[1] the queen of Goths,
She will a handmaid be to his desires,
A loving nurse, a mother to his youth.[2]

[1] *favours, elevates to empress*
[2] *be a lover, nurse and mother to the young man*

The empress and his new bride set off for the temple. They are followed by their attendants and the assembled senators, tribunes, soldiers and citizens. Titus, no longer welcome in Roman society, remains alone, bewildered at his sudden downfall:

Titus: I am not bid to wait upon[1] this bride.
Titus, when wert thou wont[2] to walk alone,
Dishonoured thus and challenged[3] of wrongs?

[1] *invited to accompany*
[2] *accustomed*
[3] *accused*

> *"Having just been at the centre of a triumphal procession, Titus suddenly finds himself alone on stage with the body of a son whom he has slain out of a mistaken sense of loyalty to the new emperor – who, at the very same moment, has gone off to marry the queen of Goths, thus further dissolving the distinction between insiders and outsiders, civilized and barbaric."*
>
> Jonathan Bate, Introduction to the Arden Shakespeare edition of *Titus Andronicus*, 2018

A glimmer of hope

Titus's brother Marcus now approaches, along with Titus's sons who had earlier helped Bassianus and Lavinia to escape. They are all appalled at Titus's impetuous killing of his son Mutius, and are determined to give the young man an honourable burial.

Titus, still aggrieved at the part they all played in preventing Lavinia's marriage to the emperor, remains adamant. Mutius must not be placed in the Andronicus family tomb, an edifice that he himself has proudly maintained and embellished:

Titus:	Traitors, away! He rests not in this tomb.
	This monument five hundred years hath stood,
	Which I have sumptuously re-edified.[1]
	Here none but soldiers and Rome's servitors
	Repose in fame; none basely slain in brawls.
	Bury him where you can, he comes not here.
Marcus:	My lord, this is impiety in you;
	My nephew Mutius' deeds do plead for him,
	He must be buried with his brethren.

[1] *rebuilt, improved*

Titus's sons join their uncle in demanding a suitable burial for Mutius in the family tomb. Titus responds angrily; his own brother is treating him disrespectfully, he complains, and his sons are failing to show the obedience due to him as their father. Eventually all of them kneel before Titus and plead with him to allow the burial to take place, appealing to his sense of morality.

Titus grudgingly agrees, but makes it clear that he is far from happy:

Marcus: [*kneeling*] Suffer[1] thy brother Marcus to inter
His noble nephew here in virtue's nest,[2]
That died in honour and Lavinia's cause.
Thou art a Roman, be not barbarous.
... Let not young Mutius then, that was thy joy,
Be barred his entrance here.

Titus: Rise, Marcus, rise.
The dismall'st day is this that e'er I saw:
To be dishonoured by my sons in Rome!
Well, bury him, and bury me the next.

[1] *allow*
[2] *this place of virtue; the family tomb*

The brothers place Mutius's body in the vault and say a brief farewell. They then depart, leaving Marcus and Titus alone together. Marcus mentions the emperor's impulsive decision to marry Tamora, the queen of the Goths. It is puzzling, agrees Titus, but the situation may work to their advantage; Tamora must surely realise that her elevation to the status of empress was ultimately brought about by Titus, the man who captured her and brought her to Rome. With luck, she will use her influence with Saturninus to see that Titus is rewarded and returned to the emperor's favour:

Marcus: How comes it that the subtle[1] queen of Goths
Is of a sudden thus advanced in Rome?

Titus: I know not, Marcus, but I know it is;[2]
Whether by device[3] or no, the heavens can tell.
Is she not then beholding to the man
That brought her for this high good turn so far?[4]

Marcus: Yes, and will nobly him remunerate.[5]

[1] *cunning, devious*
[2] *all I know is that it has happened*
[3] *scheming, trickery*
[4] *indebted to the man who brought her here, and made her good fortune possible*
[5] *reward*

Perhaps, hopes Titus, his future is not as bleak as he had feared.

A show of support

The conversation between Titus and Marcus is interrupted by a loud fanfare of trumpets, heralding the entry of the emperor Saturninus and Tamora, his new wife. They are accompanied by Tamora's two sons, Chiron and Demetrius, and her attendant Aaron.

At another door, the newlyweds Bassianus and Lavinia enter, accompanied by Titus's sons. The atmosphere is calm, but there is hostility in the air as the two parties face one another. The emperor speaks first. He addresses his brother, who replies coldly and formally, and threatens to walk away immediately:

Saturninus: So, Bassianus, you have played your prize.[1]
       God give you joy, sir, of your gallant bride.
Bassianus: And you of yours, my lord. I say no more,
       Nor wish no less, and so I take my leave.

> [1] *won this bout; achieved your aim, by marrying Lavinia*

Saturninus accuses his brother of treachery, and warns him that his abduction of Lavinia will be punished under Roman law. Bassianus insists that he was legally betrothed to Lavinia, and was entitled to rescue her from the threat of marriage to Saturninus; he is willing to defend himself in court if necessary. The emperor's response is brief but menacing:

Bassianus: … let the laws of Rome determine all;
       Meanwhile am I possessed of that[1] is mine.
Saturninus: 'Tis good, sir; you are very short with us,
       But if we live we'll be as sharp with you.[2]

> [1] *that which*
> [2] *very well; but your dismissive attitude will be met with a harsh response*

Bassianus is unmoved; he will accept death if that is the decision of a Roman court. He now speaks up for Titus, asking the emperor to take the general back into his favour. He argues that Titus was motivated by loyalty to Rome and its emperor when he made his desperate attempt to prevent Lavinia's escape, during which he killed his own son.

Titus rejects Bassianus's support. He needs no excuses for his actions, he claims, particularly from the man who helped to cause the rift between Saturninus and himself. Instead he turns directly to the emperor:

Titus: Prince Bassianus, leave to plead my deeds; [1]
'Tis thou, and those,[2] that have dishonoured me.
[*he kneels before Saturninus*] Rome and the righteous
heavens be my judge
How I have loved and honoured Saturnine.

[1] *stop trying to justify my actions; don't argue in my defence*
[2] *your companions, my sons*

'Tis thou, and those, that have dishonoured me.

"One word rings through Titus Andronicus *over and over again: honour. It appears thirty-four times in the first act alone. To an Elizabethan audience, honour was the single defining value in their idea of the Roman character ... Titus is a member of two different honour societies: Rome and the military. He lives by an inflexible sense of honour, which guides every decision he makes, on the front lines and the home front. This strict system of honour makes Titus choose Saturninus as emperor, not because he is qualified but because tradition decrees that the eldest son must succeed. Honour also guides his sacrifice of Alarbus, son of the Goths' queen, Tamora. To Titus and his family, this is an act not of revenge but of justice."*

Akiva Fox, *Dismembering Rome*, 2007

At this moment, just as Titus had hoped, Tamora intervenes. Old quarrels should be set aside, she tells her husband gently. Saturninus is taken aback:

<blockquote>

Tamora: My worthy lord, if ever Tamora
Were gracious in those princely eyes of thine,
Then hear me speak indifferently for all; [1]
And at my suit, [2] sweet, pardon what is past.

Saturninus: What, madam, be dishonoured openly,
And basely put it up [3] without revenge?

[1] *speak impartially for everyone present*
[2] *request, appeal*
[3] *accept it, submit to it*

</blockquote>

It is clear, argues Tamora, that Titus did not deliberately attempt to dishonour Saturninus. His anger at those who stole Lavinia away is clearly genuine:

<blockquote>

Tamora: ... on mine honour dare I undertake [1]
For good lord Titus' innocence in all,
Whose fury not dissembled speaks his griefs. [2]
Then at my suit look graciously on him;
Lose not so noble a friend on vain suppose, [3]
Nor with sour looks afflict his gentle heart.

[1] *give assurance*
[2] *his anger, which he is not trying to hide, shows how distressed he is*
[3] *idle speculation*

</blockquote>

If Tamora succeeds in convincing Saturninus, it seems, Titus will regain his position as a respected Roman citizen, a renowned military veteran and a close friend of the emperor.

Beneath the surface

The situation is not, however, as it appears.

When Tamora takes the emperor aside for a word in private, it immediately becomes clear that, despite her soothing words, she is in reality burning with anger at Titus and his family. She can never forget or forgive the needless slaughter of her eldest son Alarbus, mutilated and burnt to ashes as a sacrifice to the sons of Titus slain in battle. Whilst not committing her son's killing himself, Titus had allowed it to go ahead, claiming it was a religious necessity.

Tamora instructs her new husband to set his resentment aside for the time being and make a show of leniency. The people of Rome, including the senators, are likely to sympathise with Titus, she warns. Failure to restore the general to the status that he deserves could cost Saturninus his throne:

> Tamora: [aside] My lord, be ruled by me, be won at last,[1]
> Dissemble[2] all your griefs and discontents.
> You are but newly planted in your throne;
> Lest then the people, and patricians too,
> Upon a just survey take Titus' part,[3]
> And so supplant[4] you for ingratitude,
> Which Rome reputes to be a heinous sin,
> Yield at entreats[5] ...
>
> [1] allow yourself to be persuaded
> [2] disguise, hide
> [3] in case they decide to support Titus when they have considered the facts
> [4] depose, overthrow
> [5] consent to my requests

It is not just the security of their rule that Tamora has in mind. When the time is right, she will take revenge on the entire Andronicus family. She recalls bitterly how they refused to show mercy to her, a queen, when she pleaded with them on her knees for her son's life. Soon they will suffer for their insolence:

Tamora: ... let me alone: [1]
I'll find a day to massacre them all,
And raze their faction [2] and their family,
The cruel father and his traitorous sons
To whom I sued for my dear son's life,
And make them know what 'tis to let a queen
Kneel in the streets and beg for grace [3] in vain.

[1] *leave it to me*
[2] *eliminate their supporters*
[3] *mercy*

Resuming a relaxed, friendly demeanour, the empress and her husband now return to the company.

Back in the fold

Tamora guides her husband to the kneeling figure of Titus, and appeals to him to show compassion to the old general. Titus is overjoyed at the emperor's apparent change of heart:

Tamora: Come, come, sweet emperor; come, Andronicus;
Take up this good old man,[1] and cheer the heart
That dies in tempest of thy angry frown.
Saturninus: Rise, Titus, rise; my empress hath prevailed.
Titus: [*rising from his knees*] I thank your majesty and her,
       my lord;
These words, these looks, infuse new life in me.

[1] *ask Titus to rise*

Tamora now addresses Titus directly. As empress, she asserts, it is her duty to consider the good of Rome, and to advise her husband accordingly. However, Titus too must play his part:

Tamora: Titus, I am incorporate in Rome,[1]
A Roman now adopted happily,
And must advise the emperor for his good.
This day all quarrels die, Andronicus.

[1] *formally bound up with Rome; part of the body of
the state*

Turning to the others, Tamora announces that not only Titus but his whole family should be reconciled with the emperor. They will all be treated favourably, she promises, if they put aside their quarrels and ask for forgiveness. Titus's sons, his brother Marcus and his daughter Lavinia all kneel before the emperor.

Titus's eldest son Lucius apologises for the way he and his brothers forcibly took Lavinia away; they believed it was the honourable thing to do, he claims, as she was legally engaged to Bassianus. His uncle Marcus echoes the young man's plea. At first Saturninus turns his back on them, irritated by their attempts to justify themselves, but Tamora quickly brings him into line:

Tamora:	… By my advice, all humbled on your knees,
	You shall ask pardon of his majesty.
	[*Marcus, Lavinia and Titus's sons kneel*]
Lucius:	We do, and vow to heaven and to his highness
	That what we did was mildly as we might,[1]
	Tendering[2] our sister's honour and our own.
Marcus:	That on mine honour here do I protest.[3]
Saturninus:	Away, and talk not; trouble us no more.
Tamora:	Nay, nay, sweet emperor, we must all be friends.
	The tribune and his nephews kneel for grace.
	I will not be denied; sweet heart, look back.[4]

[1] *with as little force as possible*
[2] *considering, bearing in mind*
[3] *affirm, declare*
[4] *turn around, reconsider*

Prompted by Tamora, the emperor asks the supplicants to rise from their knees, and announces a general amnesty for all those involved in the recent disturbances. As a sign of his goodwill, Saturninus invites Titus and his family to feast with him.

Titus, now in high spirits, declares that they should celebrate by spending the next day hunting. He promises the emperor a day of excitement:

Titus: Tomorrow, and[1] it please your majesty
          To hunt the panther and the hart with me,
          With horn and hound we'll give your grace *bonjour.*[2]
Saturninus: Be it so, Titus, and *gramercy*[3] too.

[1] *if*
[2] *we'll rouse you in the morning with hunting-horns and hounds*
[3] *great thanks ('grand merci', echoing Titus's use of French)*

The atmosphere is one of noisy celebration as, accompanied by the blare of trumpets, the crowd follows Saturninus and his wife towards the emperor's palace.

"Titus is a man out of his normal environment. He's a soldier. He's a person who has spent the last ten years fighting the Goths. He is Rome's great champion, a man who is at home in the blood and gore of the battlefield, a man who behaves according to the strict book of military honor ... The play starts with his return to Rome, and we never actually see him on the battlefield. He is now in the world of the palace, a world where he is not at home; he is not a politician."

Director Gale Edwards on her 2007 production of *Titus Andronicus* for the Shakespeare Theatre Company, Washington D.C.

Aiming high

Tamora's attendant, Aaron the Moor, is reflecting on his mistress's dramatic change of fortunes. A short time ago, she was a prisoner in chains, but now she is the empress of Rome, all-powerful and unassailable:

Aaron: Now climbeth Tamora Olympus' top,[1]
Safe out of Fortune's shot,[2] and sits aloft,
Secure of [3] thunder's crack or lightning flash,
Advanced above pale envy's threatening reach.[4]

[1] *the peak of Mount Olympus, home of the gods*
[2] *protected from the world's misfortunes, out of harm's way*
[3] *safe from*
[4] *beyond the reach of malice or jealousy*

Aaron is determined to exploit his mistress's rise to power to the full. As he ponders his next steps, he reveals that he is more than a servant to Tamora. In fact the woman is so infatuated with him, he boasts, that the power in the relationship lies with him rather than with the empress:

Aaron: Then, Aaron, arm thy heart and fit[1] thy thoughts
To mount aloft with thy imperial mistress
And mount her pitch,[2] whom thou in triumph long
Hast prisoner held, fettered in amorous chains[3]
And faster bound to Aaron's charming eyes[4]
Than is Prometheus tied to Caucasus.[5]

[1] *prepare*
[2] *rise to the same heights as her*
[3] *who has long been your captive, shackled by her devotion to you*
[4] *more securely captivated by your spell-binding gaze*
[5] *in Greek mythology, Prometheus was eternally chained to a rock in the Caucasus mountains as punishment for stealing fire from the gods*

In Shakespeare's time the term 'Moor' was used loosely to refer to any dark-skinned individual from Africa or the Middle East. As a Moor, Aaron is an outsider both in the world of the Goths and that of Rome. He is also an eloquent, energetic example of a character frequently found in Elizabethan drama, the Machiavel:

"The Machiavel was a villainous but humorous character type, a sly cynic who loves evil for its own sake. A Machiavel is characterised by a delight in evil that makes other motivation unnecessary, the habit of commenting on his own activities in humorous soliloquies, treachery to his own allies, a tendency to lewdness, and a cynical contempt for goodness and religion ... the Machiavel takes his name from the Italian political philosopher Niccolò Machiavelli (1469-1527), who was – and is – popularly misunderstood to have advocated atheism, treachery and criminality as preferable to other means of statecraft."

Charles Boyce, *Shakespeare A to Z*, 1990

Aaron's ambitions are not just for himself, however. He intends, with Tamora's help, to bring about nothing less than the destruction of the Goths' old enemy, the Roman empire:

Aaron: Away with slavish weeds [1] and servile thoughts!
           I will be bright, and shine in pearl and gold
           To wait upon this new-made empress.
           To wait, said I? To wanton [2] with this queen,
           This goddess, this Semiramis, [3] this nymph,
           This siren [4] that will charm Rome's Saturnine
           And see his shipwreck and his commonweal's. [5]

[1] *servant's clothing*
[2] *enjoy myself, do as I please*
[3] *legendary Eastern queen, ruler of a great empire,
     famed for her beauty, cruelty and seductive powers*
[4] *bewitching sea-nymph whose singing lured sailors
     towards rocks and cliffs*
[5] *the annihilation of Saturninus and his empire*

Evil intentions

Aaron's musings are interrupted by the approach of two rowdy, argumentative young men. They are Tamora's sons, the princes Demetrius and Chiron, and it immediately becomes clear that they are both in love with the same woman. Demetrius warns off his younger brother, insisting that he is too young and foolish for the woman in question. She may, in any case, already be in love with Demetrius:

Demetrius: Chiron, thy years want wit,[1] thy wits want edge
And manners, to intrude where I am graced,
And may, for aught thou knowest, affected be.[2]

[1] *you are young and lacking in sense*
[2] *you are showing a lack of courtesy by interfering in my pursuit of a woman who favours me and, for all you know, may even be in love with me*

Chiron is annoyed that his older brother should, yet again, try to claim superiority. He has just as much right as Demetrius to pursue the woman, he argues, and is prepared to prove it with his sword if necessary. It emerges that the woman with whom the two men are infatuated is none other than Lavinia, Titus's daughter, who has just married the emperor's brother Bassianus:

Chiron: Demetrius, thou dost overween in all,
And so in this, to bear me down with braves.[1]
'Tis not the difference of a year or two
Makes me less gracious or thee more fortunate;[2]
I am as able and as fit as thou
To serve, and to deserve my mistress' grace,
And that my sword upon thee shall approve,[3]
And plead my passions for Lavinia's love.[4]

[1] *you always treat me arrogantly, as you are doing now, trying to intimidate me with your bravado*
[2] *our age difference doesn't make me less worthy of her love, or give you an advantage*
[3] *prove*
[4] *show how strong my feelings for Lavinia are*

Demetrius is scornful of his brother's attempt to threaten him; the weapon he carries is nothing more than an ornament, he claims, and he should leave it in its sheath until he is old enough to use it. Stung by the insult, Chiron draws his sword; Demetrius, in response, does the same.

Aaron, who has been observing the dispute, now intervenes. The imperial palace is not far away, he reminds them: and if word of their quarrel reached the emperor, or their mother Tamora, there would be serious trouble. The brothers continue to argue and threaten one another, and Aaron again urges them to calm down. The idea that Lavinia could be seduced away from her husband is not only absurd but dangerous, he warns:

Aaron:	Now, by the gods that warlike Goths adore,
	This petty brabble[1] will undo us all.
	Why, lords, and think you not how dangerous
	It is to jet[2] upon a prince's right?
	What, is Lavinia then become so loose,[3]
	Or Bassianus so degenerate,
	That for her love such quarrels may be broached[4]
	Without controlment, justice, or revenge?

[1] *squabble, brawl*
[2] *encroach*
[3] *debauched, immoral*
[4] *arguments over who should win Lavinia's love can be carried out openly*

To Aaron's dismay, the young men claim that they do not care who knows of their intentions. Even the threat of death does not deter them:

Aaron:	Why, are ye mad? Or know ye not in Rome
	How furious and impatient they be,
	And cannot brook[1] competitors in love?
	I tell you, lords, you do but plot your deaths
	By this device.[2]
Chiron:	Aaron, a thousand deaths
	Would I propose,[3] to achieve her whom I love.

[1] *tolerate*
[2] *idea, intention*
[3] *confront, be prepared to meet*

It soon becomes clear that it is lust rather than love that the young men feel for Lavinia. She is only a woman, Demetrius declares cynically, and any woman can be seduced whether she is married or not. Her husband need never find out:

Demetrius: Why makes thou it so strange?[1]
      She is a woman, therefore may be wooed;
      She is a woman, therefore may be won;
      She is Lavinia, therefore must be loved.
      What, man, more water glideth by the mill
      Than wots the miller of,[2] and easy it is
      Of a cut loaf to steal a shive[3] ...

[1] *why do you find it so surprising?*
[2] *more water passes by the watermill than the miller is aware of*
[3] *slice*

When Aaron realises that Demetrius and Chiron merely want to satisfy their desires, and have no interest in conducting a love affair with Lavinia, he has second thoughts. The secret abduction and rape of the virtuous Lavinia, he decides, would be a victory in his planned campaign against the hated Romans. An opportunity may present itself very soon, he tells the two young men, and they must make the most of it:

Aaron: My lords, a solemn hunting is in hand;[1]
    There will the lovely Roman ladies troop.
    The forest walks are wide and spacious,
    And many unfrequented plots[2] there are,
    Fitted by kind[3] for rape and villainy.
    Single you thither then this dainty doe,[4]
    And strike her home by force, if not by words;[5]
    This way, or not at all, stand you in hope.[6]

[1] *a celebratory hunt will take place soon*
[2] *remote, isolated areas*
[3] *nature*
[4] *select your delicate young prey and get her alone*
[5] *take her by force if you cannot persuade her with words*
[6] *this is your only hope; there is no other way*

Aaron decides to tell his mistress Tamora of the plan, confident that she will approve; she, like him, is eager to take revenge on the Romans, and the Andronicus family in particular, for the murder of her son. As he leaves, he assures Demetrius and Chiron that the hunting grounds, unlike the court, will provide the perfect setting for the planned assault:

Aaron: The emperor's court is like the house of Fame,[1]
           The palace full of tongues, of eyes and ears;
           The woods are ruthless,[2] dreadful, deaf, and dull.[3]
           There speak and strike,[4] brave boys, and take your
              turns;
           There serve your lust, shadowed from heaven's eye,
           And revel in Lavinia's treasury.[5]

           [1] a place of whispers, rumour and gossip
           [2] pitiless
           [3] oblivious
           [4] take her without hesitation
           [5] enjoy Lavinia's body to the full

Anticipation   II, ii

Outside the imperial palace, the air is filled with the blare of hunting-horns and the baying and howling of hounds: the morning of the hunt has arrived, and Titus, his sons and his brother Marcus have come to rouse the emperor.

Saturninus and Tamora emerge from the palace with their attendants. Tamora's sons, Demetrius and Chiron, come out to join them; the emperor's brother Bassianus and his new wife Lavinia complete the party.

Titus greets the emperor and his wife. It is early, remarks Saturninus, suggesting that the ladies in the group may still be drowsy. Lavinia insists that she is wide awake:

Titus: Many good morrows to your majesty;
             Madam, to you as many and as good.
             I promised your grace a hunter's peal.[1]
Saturninus: And you have rung it lustily, my lords,
             Somewhat too early for new-married ladies.
Bassianus: Lavinia, how say you?

Lavinia: I say no;
I have been broad awake two hours and more.

> [1] *the noise of hounds and horns; the hunter's*
> *equivalent of a morning peal of church bells*

There is an atmosphere of excitement among the gathering, and
the men anticipate the day's hunting with enthusiasm and pride:

Saturninus: Come on then, horse and chariots let us have,
And to our sport. [*to Tamora*] Madam, now shall ye see
Our Roman hunting.
Marcus: I have dogs, my lord,
Will rouse[1] the proudest panther in the chase,[2]
And climb the highest promontory top.
Titus: And I have horse will follow where the game
Makes way[3] and runs like swallows o'er the plain.

> [1] *that will flush out*
> [2] *royal hunting grounds*
> [3] *the prey scatters in flight*

Tamora's sons, too, are eagerly looking forward to the hunt.
However, as Demetrius remarks cryptically to his brother, they
have a different prey in mind:

Demetrius: Chiron, we hunt not, we, with horse nor hound,
But hope to pluck a dainty doe to ground.

... But hope to pluck a dainty doe to ground.

Although hunting was extremely popular in Tudor times,
Shakespeare seems to have disapproved of the activity.
Whenever he alludes to hunting, his sympathies seem to be
with the prey rather than the hunter:

"Shakespeare's images of hunting are always of deer, and
evince nothing but sympathy for the innocent, victimized
animal ... Such reactions were atypical in the sixteenth
century. Shakespeare's images are consistently sympathetic,
and this goes against the prevailing norm."

Laurie Maguire and Emma Smith, *30 Great Myths about*
Shakespeare, 2013

The victims approach

The hunt is now in progress. Aaron, on his own in a remote spot
in the forest, is carrying a bag of gold coins. He proceeds to bury
the bag at the foot of a tree, reflecting that his action would seem
odd to an unsuspecting bystander. In truth, he reveals, it is part
of a carefully prepared plot which will bring misfortune to the
gold's finder:

Aaron: He that had wit[1] would think that I had none,
To bury so much gold under a tree
And never after to inherit[2] it.
Let him that thinks of me so abjectly
Know that this gold must coin[3] a stratagem
Which, cunningly effected, will beget
A very excellent piece of villainy.
[*buries the gold*] And so repose, sweet gold, for
  their unrest
That have their alms out of the empress' chest.[4]

[1] *sense, intelligence*
[2] *recover, possess*
[3] *create, devise*
[4] *stay there, and bring unhappiness to those who
discover this gift from Tamora's treasury*

Tamora, without her attendants, now comes to join her lover.
She questions his grim expression, which is in such contrast to
their luxuriant surroundings:

Tamora: My lovely Aaron, wherefore[1] look'st thou sad
When everything doth make a gleeful boast?[2]
The birds chant melody on every bush,
The snake lies rolled[3] in the cheerful sun,
The green leaves quiver with the cooling wind
And make a chequered shadow on the ground.
Under their sweet shade, Aaron, let us sit ...

[1] *why*
[2] *is putting on a glorious display*
[3] *coiled*

Tamora is filled with an overwhelming desire is to make love to Aaron and then slumber peacefully in their shady, secluded corner. The distant sounds of the hunt, mingled with birdsong, will lull them to sleep:

> *Tamora:* ... We may, each wreathed[1] in the other's arms,
> Our pastimes[2] done, possess a golden slumber,
> Whiles hounds and horns and sweet melodious birds
> Be unto us as is a nurse's[3] song
> Of lullaby, to bring her babe asleep.
>
> [1] *entwined*
> [2] *lovemaking*
> [3] *nursemaid's*

Aaron resists her advances, declaring that his thoughts are only of taking brutal revenge on his enemies:

> *Aaron:* Madam, though Venus[1] govern your desires,
> Saturn[2] is dominator over mine ...
> Vengeance is in my heart, death in my hand,
> Blood and revenge are hammering in my head.
>
> [1] *planet associated with an amorous, passionate temperament*
> [2] *planet believed to provoke bitterness and anger*

Aaron describes the violence that he has planned. The emperor's brother is to die, while his wife Lavinia will be raped and permanently silenced:

> *Aaron:* Hark, Tamora, the empress of my soul,
> Which never hopes more heaven than rests in thee,[1]
> This is the day of doom for Bassianus;
> His Philomel must lose her tongue today,[2]
> Thy sons make pillage of her chastity,
> And wash their hands in Bassianus' blood.
>
> [1] *you, ruler of my soul, are the only heaven I can hope to achieve*
> [2] *in Greek mythology, Philomel was an Athenian princess who was abducted, raped and mutilated by her brother-in-law*

As part of his plot, Aaron has forged a letter. He hands it to Tamora, instructing her to give it to the emperor. Noticing that Bassianus and Lavinia are nearby, Aaron tells Tamora that, despite her pleas, he must leave. The newlyweds are blissfully unaware of their fate, he remarks grimly:

Aaron: Now question me no more; we are espied.
              Here comes a parcel of our hopeful booty,[1]
              Which dreads not yet[2] their lives' destruction.

[1] *part of our desired prize*
[2] *who do not yet fear*

Urging Tamora to stir up a quarrel with the approaching couple, Aaron hurries off to fetch Demetrius and Chiron, accomplices in the planned carnage.

The empress is rebuked

Bassianus and his wife, noticing the fleeing figure of Aaron, are under no illusions, and they disapprove strongly of Tamora's obvious infidelity. Bassianus suggests, sarcastically, that this may not be the emperor's wife but Diana, goddess of nature and hunting. Tamora replies sharply that they should mind their own business:

Bassianus: Who have we here? Rome's royal empress,
             Unfurnished of her well-beseeming troop?[1]
             Or is it Dian, habited like her,[2]
             Who hath abandoned her holy groves
             To see the general hunting in this forest?
Tamora: Saucy[3] controller[4] of my private steps,
             Had I the power that some say Dian had,
             Thy temples should be planted presently
             With horns, as was Actaeon's[5] ...

[1] *unaccompanied by her splendid entourage*
[2] *disguised as Tamora*
[3] *insolent*
[4] *household employee who checked domestic accounts; lackey, busybody*
[5] *when Actaeon observed Diana bathing, she transformed him into a stag, and he was torn apart by his own hounds*

It is ironic, remarks Lavinia, that Tamora should mention this particular story, as she has clearly placed a pair of horns, the traditional symbol of a cuckolded husband, on the emperor himself:

Lavinia: Under your patience,[1] gentle empress,
'Tis thought you have a goodly gift in horning,[2]
And to be doubted[3] that your Moor and you
Are singled forth[4] to try experiments.[5]

[1] by your leave; if you don't mind my saying so
[2] cuckolding, being unfaithful
[3] suspected
[4] have secluded yourselves here
[5] investigate, learn more; commit adultery

Outraged at the empress's behaviour, the couple decide to leave. Bassianus warns her that the emperor will learn of her infidelity. Lavinia adds that this is not the first time that her conduct has been called into question, and refers scathingly to her dark-skinned lover. Tamora, meanwhile, remains unmoved:

Lavinia: I pray you, let us hence,[1]
And let her joy[2] her raven-coloured[3] love;
This valley fits the purpose passing well.[4]
Bassianus: The king my brother shall have note of this.
Lavinia: Ay, for these slips have made him noted long:[5]
Good king, to be so mightily abused!
Tamora: Why, I have patience to endure all this.

[1] get away from here
[2] enjoy
[3] black
[4] this dark, shadowy place suits their depraved
    intentions very well
[5] your suspicious behaviour has made him the subject
    of gossip

At this moment Tamora's sons Demetrius and Chiron appear, sent by Aaron; and with their arrival, an air of menace descends on the scene.

Retribution

Demetrius greets his mother, remarking that she seems distressed; he has been warned by Aaron that an argument is taking place, and that she may need protection. Tamora confirms that Bassianus and Lavinia have been abusing her, and she immediately invents a tale of cruelty and wickedness. The couple lured her to this dreadful, dark corner, she claims:

Tamora: These two have 'ticed[1] me hither to this place,
A barren detested vale you see it is;
The trees, though summer, yet forlorn and lean,
O'ercome with moss and baleful[2] mistletoe;
Here never shines the sun, here nothing breeds
Unless[3] the nightly owl or fatal[4] raven.

[1] *enticed*
[2] *evil, poisonous*
[3] *except*
[4] *ominous, heralding death*

Bassianus and Lavinia intend to tie her to a tree and leave her here overnight, she says, knowing that the evil spirits that inhabit this area will drive her mad and eventually kill her. They have subjected her to a stream of insults too, she alleges, and she is thankful that her sons have come just in time to rescue her. She urges them to take action at once:

Tamora: … they called me foul adulteress,
Lascivious Goth, and all the bitterest terms
That ever ear did hear to such effect.
And had you not by wondrous fortune come,
This vengeance on me had they executed.[1]
Revenge it as you love your mother's life,
Or be ye not henceforth called my children.

[1] *they would have carried out their threat, and killed me*

Demetrius attacks Bassianus without hesitation, stabbing him violently, and Chiron, determined to prove himself, delivers the fatal blow.

Tamora, dagger in hand, now turns towards the horrified Lavinia, but Demetrius intervenes. Killing her now would not be good enough, he declares. She has always prided herself on her virtue, and her fidelity to her husband, and that self-assurance must be wiped out before she dies:

Demetrius: [*to Tamora*] Stay, madam, here is more belongs to her:[1]
First thrash the corn, then after burn the straw.[2]
This minion stood upon her chastity,[3]
Upon her nuptial vow, her loyalty,
And with that quaint hope braves your mightiness;[4]
And shall she carry this unto her grave?

[1] *she deserves more than this; we have more planned for her*
[2] *the worthless straw should not be destroyed until the goodness has been thrashed out of it*
[3] *this hussy boasted of her purity*
[4] *she defies your majesty with that pitiful hope*

Tamora agrees to the rape of Lavinia, but insists that she must not live to reveal the truth. Her sons prepare to drag their victim away:

Tamora: But when ye have the honey ye desire,
Let not this wasp outlive, us both to sting.[1]
Chiron: I warrant you, madam, we will make that sure.
[*to Lavinia*] Come, mistress, now perforce we will enjoy
That nice-preserved honesty[2] of yours.

[1] *survive, and bring about our downfall*
[2] *carefully guarded chastity*

Lavinia makes a desperate plea for mercy. Her father Titus, she reminds Tamora, brought the queen to Rome as a prisoner when he could easily have had her executed. Far from placating Tamora, however, the mention of Titus rouses her to even greater anger. His decision to allow Tamora's eldest son Alarbus to be butchered is at the root of her bitter, unforgiving fury:

Lavinia:	O, let me teach thee[1] for my father's sake,
	That gave thee life when well he might have slain thee;
	Be not obdurate, open thy deaf ears.
Tamora:	Hadst thou in person ne'er offended me,
	Even for his sake am I pitiless.[2]
	Remember, boys, I poured forth tears in vain
	To save your brother from the sacrifice,
	But fierce Andronicus would not relent.
	Therefore away with her and use her as you will:
	The worse to her, the better loved of me.[3]

[1] *tell you the meaning of pity*
[2] *even if you had never said anything to offend me, your father's deeds have banished any thoughts of pity for you*
[3] *the more pleased I shall be*

"The only locale established in Titus Andronicus *outside the walls of Rome is the forest of Act II, where the major crimes are committed. It is to be noticed that those who are most at home and effective here are Aaron and Tamora, Chiron and Demetrius ... for Lavinia, however, the forest scene is dark and evil. Within the dim light of the forest, meanings change at the whim of the observer; this is no place for the hard clear minds of the Andronici. It is, however, a natural context for Tamora's Gothic deceptions and shifts of role."*

G. K. Hunter, *Shakespeare's Earliest Tragedies,* 1974

Lavinia begs Tamora to kill her at once and save her from the violent rape that her sons intend to carry out. Tamora is unmoved, and Chiron puts his hand over Lavinia's mouth to stop any further pleas.

The young men, growing impatient, now dispose of the body of Lavinia's husband Bassianus: Aaron has prepared a deep pit nearby for the purpose, and Demetrius carries the corpse over to the pit and drops it in. The two men finally drag Lavinia away to her fate. Tamora, urging them on, hopes that further deaths will follow:

> *Tamora:* Farewell, my sons; see that you make her sure.[1]
> Ne'er let my heart know merry cheer indeed
> Till all the Andronici be made away.[2]
>
> [1] *make sure that she will never again be a threat to us*
> [2] *eradicated, killed*

Trapped

Tamora leaves, and the shady corner of the forest is deserted; only the lifeless body of Bassianus remains, at the bottom of the half-hidden pit prepared by Aaron.

The Moor himself now approaches, leading Quintus and Martius, Titus's two younger sons. There is a panther sleeping nearby, he promises, but the boys are losing interest in the hunt. Besides, the gloomy place to which Aaron has brought them makes them uneasy:

> *Aaron:* Come on, my lords, the better foot before.[1]
> Straight will I bring you to the loathsome pit
> Where I espied the panther fast asleep.
> *Quintus:* My sight is very dull, whate'er it bodes.[2]
> *Martius:* And mine, I promise you; were it not for shame,[3]
> Well could I leave our sport to sleep awhile.
>
> [1] *press on, keep going*
> [2] *everything looks dim, which doesn't bode well*
> [3] *if it weren't a shameful thing to do*

Martius suddenly disappears: guided by Aaron, he has fallen into the pit containing Bassianus's body. Quintus approaches the pit tentatively, and is aghast to find that the foliage covering the entrance is bloodstained. Martius calls for help, but Quintus is reluctant to come too close, sensing that the pit is an evil, perilous place:

Martius:	Why dost not comfort me and help me out
	From this unhallowed[1] and bloodstained hole?
Quintus:	I am surprised with an uncouth fear;[2]
	A chilling sweat o'erruns my trembling joints;
	My heart suspects more than mine eye can see.

[1] *unholy, abhorrent*
[2] *overwhelmed by a strange, unfamiliar fear*

There is a corpse in the pit, Martius tells his brother. A ring on the dead man's hand contains a gem that is glowing faintly, lighting up the man's face: Martius recognises him as the emperor's brother Bassianus.

Quintus finally plucks up the courage to approach the mouth of the pit. He reaches down and manages to grasp his brother's hand: but he does not have the strength to pull Martius up, and Martius, faint with fear and shock, is too weak to climb out. Eventually Quintus is dragged down into the pit with his brother.

An incriminating letter

Aaron, meanwhile, has left the boys to their fate: he has fetched the emperor, confident that Titus's sons will be blamed for the death of Bassianus. At first, the emperor refuses to believe that his brother is dead:

> *Saturninus:* [*speaking into the pit*] Say, who art thou that lately
> didst descend
> Into this gaping hollow of the earth?
> *Martius:* The unhappy sons of old Andronicus,
> Brought hither in a most unlucky hour
> To find thy brother Bassianus dead.
> *Saturninus:* My brother dead? I know thou dost but jest;
> He and his lady both are at the lodge
> Upon the north side of this pleasant chase.[1]
> 'Tis not an hour since I left them there.
>
> [1] *hunting ground*

Martius repeats that Bassianus's corpse is indeed in the pit. At this moment, just as Saturninus realises that the devastating news is true, Tamora arrives, along with Titus and his eldest son Lucius.

Tamora reveals that she has discovered, too late, a plot to kill Bassianus. She produces the letter earlier forged by Aaron: it appears to give instructions to an assassin to kill Bassianus on the day of the hunt if the conspirators fail to do so themselves. There is a reward, the writers promise, buried nearby. Tamora hands the letter to the emperor, who reads it to the gathering:

> *Saturninus:* 'And if we miss to meet him handsomely,[1]
> Sweet huntsman – Bassianus 'tis we mean –
> Do thou so much as dig the grave for him;
> Thou know'st our meaning. Look for thy reward
> Among the nettles at the elder tree
> Which overshades the mouth of that same pit
> Where we decreed[2] to bury Bassianus.'
>
> [1] *if we do not come across him and kill him ourselves*
> [2] *decided, agreed*

Perhaps the intended assassin is still in the vicinity, says Saturninus, although he was evidently not required; the conspirators have clearly carried out the murder themselves, and have just taken the body down into the pit. As further proof, Aaron, delving under the nearby tree, announces that he has found the bag of gold mentioned in the letter.

The emperor turns to Titus, denouncing his sons for the brutal murder of Bassianus. Tamora declares her satisfaction that the culprits have been identified so easily and conclusively:

Saturninus: Two of thy whelps, fell curs of bloody kind,[1]
Have here bereft my brother of his life.
Sirs, drag them from the pit unto the prison.
There let them bide[2] until we have devised
Some never-heard-of torturing pain for them.
Tamora: What, are they in this pit? O wondrous thing!
How easily murder is discovered!

[1] *young pups, cruel hounds of a bloodthirsty nature*
[2] *wait, stay*

Bassianus's body is brought up from the pit, along with the two young suspects. Titus kneels before the emperor and attempts to plead on his sons' behalf. He asks to be allowed to keep them in his custody, whether or not they are guilty, until they face trial. Saturninus dismisses his pleas out of hand, determined to see the young men punished as severely as possible.

As Saturninus strides away angrily, Tamora approaches Titus. She assures him, sympathetically, that she will do what she can to influence her husband and save the young men's lives:

Saturninus: Let them not speak a word: the guilt is plain;
For, by my soul, were there worse end than death[1]
That end upon them should be executed.
Tamora: Andronicus, I will entreat[2] the king;
Fear not[3] thy sons, they shall do well enough.

[1] *if there were some punishment worse than death*
[2] *plead with, appeal to*
[3] *have no fear for*

A silent victim

Demetrius and Chiron have, as they threatened, raped Lavinia: and to ensure that her attackers will never be named, they have cut out her tongue and hacked off her hands. The young men are in high spirits, and they taunt her cruelly, mocking her inability to communicate:

Demetrius:	So now go tell, an if thy tongue can speak,
	Who 'twas that cut thy tongue and ravished thee.
Chiron:	Write down thy mind, bewray thy meaning so,[1]
	An if thy stumps will let thee play the scribe.

[1] *reveal your thoughts in writing*

Lavinia cannot even call for help, the young men remark jeeringly. They disregard Tamora's instruction to kill their victim. In their eyes, Lavinia is now nothing more than a harmless figure of fun, and they leave her to wander the forest alone:

Chiron:	Go home, call for sweet[1] water, wash thy hands.
Demetrius:	She hath no tongue to call, nor hands to wash,
	And so let's leave her to her silent walks.
Chiron:	An 'twere my cause[2] I should go hang myself.
Demetrius:	If thou hadst hands to help thee knit[3] the cord.

[1] *perfumed*
[2] *if I were in her situation*
[3] *knot*

As Lavinia stands in silent anguish, she hears the blare of a hunting-horn, and tries to run away as a huntsman approaches. The lone hunter is Titus's brother Marcus, and as he catches up with Lavinia he realises, to his horror, that her hands have been cut off:

Marcus:	Who is this? My niece, that flies away so fast?
	Cousin,[1] a word. Where is your husband?
	[*Lavinia stops and turns towards him*] If I do dream,
	would all my wealth would wake me;[2]

If I do wake, some planet strike me down [3]
That I may slumber an eternal sleep!
Speak, gentle niece …

[1] *relative, niece*
[2] *I would give everything I own to wake from this*
   nightmare
[3] *may some fateful planet use its deadly influence to*
   kill me

Lavinia opens her mouth, and Marcus's horror is redoubled as a stream of blood reveals that her tongue has been cut out. He realises immediately what has happened, and is filled with impotent fury, knowing that Lavinia cannot name her attackers.

No man who knew Lavinia's true nature could have done such a thing, Marcus tells himself, as he recalls her grace and delicacy as a musician:

Marcus: O, had the monster seen those lily hands
        Tremble like aspen leaves [1] upon a lute
        And make the silken strings delight to kiss them,
        He would not then have touched them for his life.
        Or had he heard the heavenly harmony
        Which that sweet tongue hath made,
        He would have dropped his knife and fell asleep,
        As Cerberus at the Thracian poet's feet. [2]

   [1] *move swiftly and daintily, like leaves fluttering in*
      the breeze
   [2] *in Greek mythology, the Thracian bard Orpheus*
      could charm and pacify animals with his music,
      including Cerberus, the monstrous three-headed
      dog that guarded the gates of the underworld

Marcus leads Lavinia away to join her father Titus; even though he will be devastated, he must know what has happened to his only daughter.

> *... the heavenly harmony*
> *Which that sweet tongue hath made ...*

Marcus's lengthy, ornate speech when he is confronted by Lavinia – where the stage direction reads '*her hands cut off and her tongue cut out, and ravished*' – can seem impossibly inappropriate to modern audiences, and the speech is often cut by directors. Some critics have suggested that Shakespeare's intention is to highlight the limits of language in the face of unbearable suffering:

> *"With the re-appearance of Lavinia, and her discovery by her instinctually poetic uncle, the inadequacy of symbolic language to distil the horrific experience of what has happened to her is laid bare."*

> Harry R. McCarthy, Introduction to the New Oxford Shakespeare edition of *Titus Andronicus*, 2025

The depths of despair   III, i

Titus's sons Quintus and Martius, wrongly convicted of the murder of the emperor's brother Bassianus, are being led to their execution. Their father is pleading desperately for mercy, but he is ignored by the solemn procession of senators and judges accompanying them. Titus reminds the dignitaries of his lifelong service to the state:

Titus: Hear me, grave fathers; noble tribunes, stay!
        For pity of mine age, whose youth was spent
        In dangerous wars whilst you securely slept;
        For all my blood in Rome's great quarrel[1] shed,
        For all the frosty nights that I have watched,[2]
        And for these bitter tears which now you see
        Filling the aged wrinkles in my cheeks,
        Be pitiful to my condemned sons ...

[1] *cause*
[2] *stayed on guard*

He did not weep for the death of his other sons, says Titus, as they died in battle. These two, by contrast, are to be put to death for a dishonourable act, but Titus is convinced that they are not innately wicked, and that they deserve to be shown mercy. He prostrates himself before the judges as he speaks; and he continues pleading even when the procession has passed and no one is left to hear him.

Lucius, Titus's eldest son, now approaches. He is distressed to see his father lying alone, lamenting, on the stony ground, and gently points out that the tribunes and judges have moved on. It makes no difference, Titus replies despondently:

Lucius: My gracious lord, no tribune hears you speak.
Titus: Why, 'tis no matter, man: if they did hear,
          They would not mark me,[1] or if they did mark
          They would not pity me; yet plead I must,
          And bootless unto them.[2]
          Therefore I tell my sorrows to the stones,
          Who, though they cannot answer my distress,
          Yet in some sort[3] they are better than the tribunes
          For that they will not intercept[4] my tale …

[1] *take any notice of me*
[2] *even if it has no influence on the judges*
[3] *in a way*
[4] *interrupt*

Stones are silent and harmless, reflects Titus, unlike the hard-hearted politicians of Rome who, with a word, can condemn a man to death. When Lucius reveals that he has been banished from Rome for attempting to free his two brothers, Titus rises from the ground and congratulates him, believing that no member of the Andronicus family is safe in Rome any longer:

Titus: O happy man, they have befriended thee!
          Why, foolish Lucius, dost thou not perceive
          That Rome is but a wilderness of tigers?
          Tigers must prey, and Rome affords no prey
          But me and mine.[1]

[1] *we are the only suitable victims for the predatory
   politicians of Rome*

At this moment Marcus arrives, leading the unfortunate Lavinia. Lucius collapses, devastated at the sight of his mutilated sister. Titus, already filled with resentment towards his ungrateful homeland and becoming increasingly irrational, is overwhelmed:

Titus: Speak, Lavinia, what accursed hand
Hath made thee handless in thy father's sight?
... My grief was at the height before thou cam'st,
And now like Nilus it disdaineth bounds.[1]
Give me a sword, I'll chop off my hands too,
For they have fought for Rome, and all in vain ...

[1] *it overflows, like the flooding river Nile*

Lucius, recovering, asks who committed this dreadful crime. Marcus explains that Lavinia was in this appalling state when he found her wandering in the forest, unable to name her assailants. This latest calamity leaves Titus heartbroken, and he fears that his torment is more than he can bear:

Titus: ... now I stand as one upon a rock,
Environed[1] with a wilderness of sea,
Who marks the waxing[2] tide grow wave by wave,
Expecting ever when some envious surge
Will in his brinish bowels swallow him.[3]

[1] *surrounded*
[2] *rising*
[3] *waiting for a hateful torrent to drag me into the ocean at any moment*

Titus laments the depths of suffering to which his entire family has fallen:

Titus: This way to death my wretched sons[1] are gone;
Here stands my other son, a banished man,
And here my brother, weeping at my woes;
But that which gives my soul the greatest spurn[2]
Is dear Lavinia, dearer than my soul.

[1] *Quintus and Martius, who have just passed by on their way to the place of execution*
[2] *scornful kick, blow*

As the full horror of Lavinia's plight dawns on Titus, he is filled with pity for his only daughter. As well as her terrible injuries, she must contend with the deaths of both her husband Bassianus and her brothers:

Titus: Thou hast no hands to wipe away thy tears,
           Nor tongue to tell me who hath martyred thee; [1]
           Thy husband he is dead, and for his death
           Thy brothers are condemned, and dead by this.[2]

           [1] *caused your suffering*
           [2] *by now*

At the mention of her brothers, Lavinia starts weeping. For a moment, Titus wonders whether they really were guilty of the murder of Bassianus, but he quickly dismisses the thought; it must be the news of their unjust execution that has upset her. Titus is desperate to console his daughter, but realises he can do nothing to help her. He is left sobbing, helpless, and almost mad with grief.

Titus Andronicus was hugely successful during Shakespeare's lifetime, and was performed regularly for over twenty years following its first performances in 1594. It fell out of favour with later generations, however, and many scholars – even those who admired Shakespeare – began to doubt whether this gruesome play was genuinely the work of the Bard. One such critic was the famous Dr Johnson, who expressed his doubts in his edition of the complete works of Shakespeare:

"The colour of the style is wholly different from that of the other plays ... The barbarity of the spectacles, and the general massacre which are here exhibited, can scarcely be conceived tolerable to any audience."

Samuel Johnson, *The Plays of William Shakespeare*, 1765

Sacrifice

At this moment a dark figure approaches the group. Aaron –
who, unbeknownst to them, lies behind the family's misfortunes
– has come with a message from the emperor. Saturninus has
made Titus an offer, Aaron tells him. His sons' lives can be
spared, but at a terrible cost:

> *Aaron:*   Titus Andronicus, my lord the emperor
> Sends thee this word: that if thou love thy sons,
> Let Marcus, Lucius, or thyself, old Titus,
> Or any one of you, chop off your hand
> And send it to the king; he for the same
> Will send thee hither both thy sons alive,
> And that shall be the ransom for their fault.[1]

> [1] *payment for their crime, blood money*

Far from being shocked by the grisly proposition, Titus is
overjoyed. He accepts the offer without hesitation, ecstatic at the
prospect of seeing his sons again, and indifferent to any pain or
suffering that may result:

> *Titus:*   O gracious emperor, O gentle[1] Aaron!
> Did ever raven sing so like a lark
> That gives sweet tidings of the sun's uprise?
> With all my heart I'll send the emperor my hand.
> Good Aaron, wilt thou help to chop it off?

> [1] *kind, generous*

Lucius now intervenes. He declares that his father is a heroic
general, a veteran of countless battles against Rome's enemies,
and does not deserve to suffer in this way. It is he, the younger
man, who should make this sacrifice:

> *Lucius:*   Stay, father, for that noble hand of thine
> That hath thrown down so many enemies
> Shall not be sent. My hand will serve the turn;[1]
> My youth can better spare my blood than you,
> And therefore mine shall save my brothers' lives.

> [1] *serve the purpose, satisfy the need*

Titus's brother Marcus overrules his nephew: Lucius, like his father, has fought bravely for Rome, and neither he nor Titus should lose their hand. As a politician, Marcus admits, he has never needed to display physical courage, but it is fitting that he should do so now:

Marcus: Which of your hands hath not defended Rome
            And reared aloft the bloody battle-axe,
            Writing destruction on the enemy's casque?[1]
            O, none of both but are of high desert.[2]
            My hand hath been but idle;[3] let it serve
            To ransom my two nephews from their death,
            Then have I kept it to a worthy end.[4]

            [1] *helmet*
            [2] *you have both performed admirable deeds*
            [3] *useless, ineffectual*
            [4] *it will at last have served a valuable purpose*

As the three men argue, Aaron grows impatient. The execution may take place at any minute, he warns, and a decision must be made soon:

Aaron: Nay, come, agree whose hand shall go along,
            For fear they die before their pardon come.

Nay, come, agree whose hand shall go along ...

There are undoubtedly moments in *Titus Andronicus* when audiences are as likely to laugh as to gasp in horror:

"The lesson of classical literature was that tragedy should be kept apart from comedy, high art from low ... but in Titus, *Shakespeare wantonly flouts the classical rules. He recognizes that there is actually a very narrow borderline between tragedy and farce. Four hundred years before the* enfants terribles *of modern Hollywood, he saw that audiences love the shock of the rollercoaster ride from violence to humour."*

Jonathan Bate, Introduction to the RSC Shakespeare edition of *Titus Andronicus*, 2011

The clamour continues, however, as Titus, Lucius and Marcus are all determined to offer their hand in exchange for the young men's lives. Finally Titus announces that he will spare his own hand, and let the other two decide between them.

Lucius and Marcus, still quarrelling, leave to fetch an axe. It now emerges that Titus has misled them; he is indeed resolved to give his own hand, and urges Aaron to cut it off while the others are out of the way. Eager to comply, Aaron draws his scimitar. Remarking secretly that he is amused at Titus's ploy, he hints that he himself is involved in a different kind of deception. A moment later, the blade comes down:

Titus:	Come hither, Aaron. I'll deceive them both;
	Lend me thy hand,[1] and I will give thee mine.
	[*he holds out his hand*]
Aaron:	[*aside*] If that be called deceit, I will be honest,[2]
	And never whilst I live deceive men so.
	But I'll deceive you in another sort,[3]
	And that you'll say [4] ere half an hour pass.
	[*he cuts off Titus's hand*]

[1] *help me to perform the deed*
[2] *if that is considered deceitful, I'll stick to honesty*
[3] *in a different way*
[4] *you'll know what I mean*

In 1955, director Peter Brook achieved great success with his production of *Titus Andronicus* at Stratford-upon-Avon. The play's violence was stylised rather than graphic; red ribbons were used rather than fake blood, for example, and the hand-cutting was concealed from the audience. However, the off-stage sound effect of crunching bone as Aaron's scimitar came down proved too much for some spectators. "At least three people pass out nightly," confirmed one theatre official. "Twenty fainted at one performance. Ten swooned last Friday."

Lucius and Marcus return with an axe, each of them determined to carry out the dreadful sacrifice proposed by the emperor. There is no longer any need to argue, Titus reveals; the deed has already been done. He gives his severed hand to Aaron, asking that it be treated with respect:

Titus: Good Aaron, give his majesty my hand;
                 Tell him it was a hand that warded [1] him
                 From thousand dangers; bid him bury it.
                 More hath it merited; that let it have. [2]
                 As for my sons, say I account of them
                 As jewels purchased at an easy [3] price,
                 And yet dear too, because I bought mine own. [4]

[1] *guarded, protected*
[2] *it deserves more than a simple burial, but let it at least have that honour*
[3] *low, cheap*
[4] *at the same time, the price was high, as what I was paying for was already mine*

Aaron takes the hand and leaves, assuring Titus that his sons will be with him soon. As he goes, however, he secretly reveals the shocking truth. His supposed offer from the emperor was a complete fabrication: there was never any question of a pardon, and the execution of Quintus and Martius is a foregone conclusion. Aaron can scarcely contain his delight at the cruel trick he has played on his unsuspecting Roman enemy:

Aaron: I go, Andronicus; and for thy hand
                 Look by and by [1] to have thy sons with thee.
                 [*aside*] Their heads, I mean. O how this villainy
                 Doth fat me with the very thoughts of it! [2]

[1] *expect soon*
[2] *just thinking about my ruse fills me with pleasure*

Sworn to vengeance

Titus, racked with pain and still in distress at his daughter's suffering, kneels and lifts his remaining hand to the heavens. Lavinia too kneels, and silently prays alongside him. As Titus weeps at the terrible, wanton cruelty inflicted on her, Marcus urges him to remain stoical and restrain his emotions.

At this moment a messenger arrives. Titus had believed that the sacrifice of his hand would save his two sons; that belief, the messenger now reveals with a heavy heart, was an illusion. He produces a macabre group of objects, and a wave of horror sweeps through the gathering:

> *Messenger:* Worthy Andronicus, ill art thou repaid
> For that good hand thou sent'st the emperor.
> Here are the heads of thy two noble sons,
> And here's thy hand in scorn to thee sent back:
> Thy grief their sports, thy resolution mocked [1] ...
>
> [1] *the emperor and his court are enjoying your grief, and making fun of your determination to save your sons*

Marcus is the first to respond, his stoicism shattered by the devastating spectacle of the severed heads and hand:

> *Marcus:* Now let hot Etna cool in Sicily,
> And be my heart an ever-burning hell! [1]
> These miseries are more than may be borne.
>
> [1] *let the heat of the volcano enter my heart and burn there forever*

Lucius, crushed at the sight of his brothers' heads, finds it hard to believe that he himself is still alive:

Lucius:	Ah, that this sight should make so deep a wound,
	And yet detested life not shrink thereat! [1]
	That ever death should let life bear his name,
	Where life hath no more interest but to breathe! [2]

> [1] *it seems impossible that my life, now worthless,*
>   *should continue after such a deep wound*
> [2] *how can life still be called life when it becomes a*
>   *living death, consisting merely of breathing?*

Titus, feeling that he is trapped in a living nightmare, is rendered almost speechless by this latest outrage. His brother urges him to grasp the true horror of the situation and express his anger. The time for patient endurance has gone:

Titus:	When will this fearful slumber have an end?
Marcus:	Now farewell flattery, die Andronicus: [1]
	Thou dost not slumber. See thy two sons' heads,
	Thy warlike hand, thy mangled daughter here,
	Thy other banished son with this dear sight [2]
	Struck pale and bloodless, and thy brother, I,
	Even like a stony image, cold and numb.
	Ah, now no more will I control [3] thy griefs:
	Rend off [4] thy silver hair ...

> [1] *stop deluding yourself; let the old Andronicus die*
> [2] *by this dire spectacle*
> [3] *try to restrain*
> [4] *tear out*

Titus does not give way to his feelings, however: to the bewilderment of his family, he starts laughing as if his cares were over. Grief and rage are of no use to him any more, he declares, as they would distract him from his true aim:

Titus:	... I have not another tear to shed.
	Besides, this sorrow is an enemy
	And would usurp upon my watery eyes
	And make them blind with tributary tears. [1]
	Then which way shall I find Revenge's cave?

> [1] *if I paid tribute to sorrow with tears, I would be*
>   *blinded and unable to pursue my goal*

From this moment onwards only one thing matters, vows Titus, surveying the severed heads of his two sons:

Titus: … these two heads do seem to speak to me
                And threat[1] me I shall never come to bliss
                Till all these mischiefs be returned again,
                Even in their throats that hath committed them.[2]

                [1] warn
                [2] until all these crimes are revenged with the utmost
                severity upon those who have committed them

Titus gathers his three family members, Marcus, Lavinia and Lucius, around him, and they all take a solemn vow to avenge the wrongs they have suffered. Titus holds one of the severed heads, and Marcus the other; Lavinia too must take part, and Titus instructs her to take his severed hand between her teeth.

"In a cruel trick, Aaron proposes a trade that would appeal to the honour-bound Titus' sense of proportion: this famous warrior's honourable hand in exchange for his sons' lives. Instead, he receives their heads, and his severed hand is scornfully returned. Their bodies and honour system mangled and devalued, the shattered Andronicus family literally picks up the pieces and begins to plot their revenge."

Akiva Fox, Dismembering Rome, 2007

Lucius, Titus's last remaining son, has been banished from Rome by the emperor Saturninus. Titus orders him to leave at once, as he is in imminent danger. In the fight against the brutal emperor and his court, Titus has decided, Lucius can play his part by enlisting the help of their old enemy:

Titus: As for thee, boy, go get thee from my sight;
            Thou art an exile, and thou must not stay;
            Hie[1] to the Goths and raise an army there,
            And if ye love me, as I think you do,
            Let's kiss and part, for we have much to do.

[1] *make your way, hurry*

A melancholy supper   III, ii

In the dining-room of Titus's house, a meal has been prepared. Titus and his brother Marcus are present, as well as his daughter Lavinia. Lucius has gone into exile, but his young son – also known as Lucius – remains with Titus.

The constant anxiety and turmoil that Titus is undergoing have produced a physical pain around his heart that he tries to force down with his remaining hand. Lavinia, he laments, cannot do the same:

Titus: This poor right hand of mine
            Is left to tyrannise[1] upon my breast,
            Who, when my heart, all mad with misery,
            Beats in this hollow prison of my flesh,
            Then thus I thump it down. [*he beats his chest*]
            [*to Lavinia*] Thou map[2] of woe, that thus dost talk
              in signs,
            When thy poor heart beats with outrageous beating,
            Thou canst not strike it thus to make it still.

[1] *attack, hit violently*
[2] *representation, image*

Marcus urges his brother to speak more reassuringly to Lavinia. Titus, becoming ever more agitated, explains that he is gradually learning to interpret her silent gestures. As he feeds her, he suspects that she is thirsty; soon, he claims, he will understand every movement she makes:

Titus: Come, let's fall to;[1] and gentle girl, eat this.
                [to the servants] Here is no drink! ...
                Speechless complainer, I will learn thy thought.
                In thy dumb action will I be as perfect [2]
                As begging hermits in their holy prayers.[3]
                Thou shalt not sigh, nor hold thy stumps to heaven,
                Nor wink, nor nod, nor kneel, nor make a sign,
                But I of these will wrest an alphabet [4]
                And by still[5] practice learn to know thy meaning.

                [1] *start our meal*
                [2] *expert, well versed*
                [3] *solitary monks who recite prayers continually, and
                    know them by heart*
                [4] *none of your gestures will escape my notice; I will
                    make sense of them all*
                [5] *constant*

Young Lucius, upset to see his grandfather so troubled, asks him to choose a more cheerful subject. Marcus pities the child, who is too young to cope with such unhappiness:

Young Lucius: Good grandsire, leave these bitter deep laments;
                Make my aunt[1] merry with some pleasing tale.
Marcus: Alas, the tender boy, in passion moved,
                Doth weep to see his grandsire's heaviness.[2]

                [1] *Lavinia*
                [2] *sadness, dejection*

Titus notices his brother make a sudden movement. When Marcus tells him that he has just killed a fly with his knife, Titus reacts with fury:

Titus: Out on thee, murderer! Thou kill'st my heart.
                Mine eyes are cloyed with view of tyranny;[1]

A deed of death done on the innocent
Becomes not [2] Titus' brother. Get thee gone ...

[1] *I cannot bear the sight of oppression*
[2] *is not fitting for*

The dead fly had parents, says Titus mournfully, and a life of his
own; he was a tiny, delicate creature who caused harm to no
one as he flew here and there, buzzing tunefully. Marcus tries to
calm his brother by likening the fly to Aaron. At this suggestion,
Titus's mood changes in an instant. He grabs the knife himself,
and starts stabbing at the dead fly frantically:

Marcus:	Pardon me, sir, it was a black ill-favoured [1] fly,
	Like to the empress' Moor; [2] therefore I killed him.
Titus:	Oh, Oh, Oh!
	Then pardon me for reprehending thee,
	For thou hast done a charitable deed.
	Give me thy knife; I will insult on him, [3]
	Flattering myself as if [4] it were the Moor
	Come hither purposely to poison me.
	[*striking at the fly*] There's for thyself, and that's
	for Tamora!

[1] *ugly*
[2] *Aaron*
[3] *triumph over him, treat him with contempt*
[4] *pleasing myself by believing*

Marcus observes his brother's erratic behaviour with sadness
and compassion. He realises that Titus's anguish is so great that
he is losing touch with reality:

Marcus:	[*aside*] Alas, poor man! Grief has so wrought on [1] him
	He takes false shadows for true substances.

[1] *worked on, affected*

The meal is over, declares Titus, and it is time to retire. Taking
his daughter to her room, he promises to comfort her by reading
her sad stories from times gone by. His eyes are growing weak
with age, he complains, so he asks young Lucius to join them;
when Titus can no longer cope, the boy can read in his place.

A strange situation is unfolding in Titus's house: young Lucius, carrying an armful of books, is being pursued by his aunt Lavinia. Disturbed by her behaviour, and unsure of what she wants, the boy is running away, and in his agitation he drops his books on the floor. At this moment Titus and Marcus enter, and he runs into their arms. They reassure him that there is nothing to worry about:

> *Young Lucius:* Help, grandsire, help! My aunt Lavinia
> Follows me everywhere, I know not why.
> Good uncle Marcus, see how swift she comes.
> Alas, sweet aunt, I know not what you mean.
> *Marcus:* Stand by me, Lucius; do not fear thine aunt.
> *Titus:* She loves thee, boy, too well to do thee harm.

Although he knows that his aunt loves him, Lucius is uneasy. He has no idea why she is so desperate to attract his attention, and fears that she has become deranged with sorrow:

> *Marcus:* Canst thou not guess wherefore she plies thee thus? [1]
> *Young Lucius:* My lord, I know not, I, nor can I guess,
> Unless some fit of frenzy do possess her;
> For I have heard my grandsire say full oft
> Extremity of griefs would make men mad ...
>
> [1] *why she is trying so persistently to communicate with you*

Eventually the boy calms down and, guided by his uncle, approaches Lavinia. She is trying to sort through the books that Lucius dropped a moment ago, and appears to be drawn to one volume in particular; it is a book of tales from mythology, explains Lucius, given to him by his mother, now dead. At the same time, Lavinia seems to be indicating something with her mutilated arms. Her meaning is not yet clear:

> *Titus:* Why lifts she up her arms in sequence thus?
> *Marcus:* I think she means that there were more than one
> Confederate in the fact; [1] ay, more there was;
> Or else to heaven she heaves them for revenge.

Titus: Lucius, what book is that she tosseth so?[2]
Young Lucius: Grandsire, 'tis Ovid's *Metamorphosis*;
              My mother gave it me.
Marcus: For love of her that's gone,
              Perhaps she culled it from among the rest.[3]

      [1] *who took part in the crime*
      [2] *is desperately trying to open*
      [3] *perhaps she has chosen it in memory of Lucius's
          mother*

Titus helps his daughter to turn over the pages, and it becomes clear that she is trying to draw their attention to Ovid's story of Philomela, a tragic tale of abduction and rape. Titus and Marcus now realise, to their horror, that Lavinia has been raped as well as savagely maimed:

Titus: What would she[1] find? Lavinia, shall I read?
              This is the tragic tale of Philomel,
              And treats of Tereus' treason and his rape;
              And rape, I fear, was root of thy annoy.[2]
Marcus: See, brother, see; note how she quotes the leaves.[3]
Titus: Lavinia, wert thou thus surprised, sweet girl,
              Ravished and wronged as Philomela was,
              Forced[4] in the ruthless,[5] vast and gloomy woods?
              [*Lavinia nods*] See, see!
              Ay, such a place there is where we did hunt ...

      [1] *is she trying to*
      [2] *the source of your anguish*
      [3] *examines the pages intently*
      [4] *raped*
      [5] *pitiless*

Titus asks Lavinia to give a sign of some kind to identify her attacker, wondering for a moment whether it was the emperor himself who committed the crime. Marcus then has an idea: he picks up his staff and, holding it in his mouth and guiding it with his feet, manages to write his name on a sandy area of the floor. He urges Lavinia to do the same, and as she does so the names of the culprits are slowly revealed: they are the sons of the empress herself, Demetrius and Chiron.

Marcus and Titus have already vowed to take revenge on the emperor and his court for the execution of Titus's two sons; now their resolve grows even stronger. Whatever the cost, Tamora's sons must die, declares Marcus, and the whole family joins him in his oath:

Marcus: My lord, kneel down with me; Lavinia, kneel;
And kneel, sweet boy, the Roman Hector's hope,[1]
And swear with me ...
That we will prosecute by good advice[2]
Mortal revenge upon these traitorous Goths,
And see their blood, or die with this reproach.[3]

   [1] *the future hero of Rome, like the legendary Hector
   who was the greatest warrior of Troy*
   [2] *pursue with a carefully considered strategy*
   [3] *die with the dishonour of failing to strike back*

Titus warns his brother that killing Demetrius and Chiron will not be easy. Their mother is fiercely protective, and has the power of the emperor behind her:

Titus: 'Tis sure enough, and you knew how.[1]
But if you hunt these bear-whelps,[2] then beware:
The dam[3] will wake, and if she wind ye[4] once
She's with the lion[5] deeply still in league ...

   [1] *it can be done, if you know how*
   [2] *cubs*
   [3] *mother*
   [4] *gets wind of you, learns of your intentions*
   [5] *Saturninus*

Wary of attempting to act directly against Tamora's sons, Titus appears to have a more underhand plot in mind. The first step, surprisingly, will be to give a gift to the two young men: his grandson Lucius is to present them with the finest weapons from Titus's armoury. Marcus, meanwhile, must refrain from taking any action himself.

Titus leaves to select the weapons, taking Lucius with him. Marcus is dismayed at the idea of giving a gift to Lavinia's attackers. This is yet another sign, he believes, of the mental turmoil that Titus's suffering has caused. He calls out to the gods to punish the offenders if Titus fails to do so himself:

Marcus:	O heavens, can you hear a good man groan
	And not relent or not compassion[1] him?
	Marcus, attend him in his ecstasy[2]
	That hath more scars of sorrow in his heart
	Than foemen's marks[3] upon his battered shield,
	But yet so just[4] that he will not revenge.
	Revenge the heavens[5] for old Andronicus!

[1] *show compassion to*
[2] *I must look after him during this fit of madness*
[3] *dents from his enemies' weapons*
[4] *righteous, principled*
[5] *may the heavens take revenge*

Revenge the heavens for old Andronicus!

In Shakespeare's time, the 'revenge play' was an extremely popular genre of drama. Such plays tended to be spectacular and bloody affairs featuring murders, violence, lawlessness and retribution; in some ways they were the equivalent of today's horror movies.

Titus Andronicus certainly falls into this category, but despite its success Shakespeare did not write any more plays of this kind. The theme of revenge is central to *Hamlet*, written several years later, but its treatment there is far more complex and nuanced than in a typical revenge play.

Revenge was a controversial topic at the time, and the morality of taking personal revenge, rather than relying on the law or on divine punishment, was a hotly debated issue. The church and the state remained firmly against private acts of revenge. The views of statesman and philosopher Francis Bacon, Shakespeare's contemporary, were typical in this respect:

"Revenge is a kind of wild justice; which the more man's nature runs to, the more ought law to weed it out ... Certainly, in taking revenge, a man is but even with his enemy; but in passing it over, he is superior; for it is a prince's part to pardon ... Vindictive persons live the life of witches who, as they are mischievous, so end they unfortunate."

Francis Bacon, *Of Revenge*, 1625

A new arrival

Young Lucius, as instructed by his grandfather Titus, has come to present the empress's sons with a gift. Aaron, the empress's attendant and secret lover, is present with the two young men. The boy addresses them formally, but struggles to hide his revulsion:

Young Lucius: My lords, with all the humbleness I may,
I greet your honours from Andronicus –
[*aside*] And pray the Roman gods confound you both.
Demetrius: Gramercy,[1] lovely Lucius. What's the news?
Young Lucius: [*aside*] That you are both deciphered,[2] that's the news,
For villains marked with rape.
[*to Chiron and Demetrius*]   May it please you,
My grandsire, well advised,[3] hath sent by me
The goodliest weapons of his armoury
To gratify your honourable youth,
The hope of Rome ...

[1] *many thanks*
[2] *discovered, identified*
[3] *after careful consideration*

With a last scornful aside, Lucius leaves, and the young men examine their gift. Wrapped around the bundle of weapons is a scroll containing a brief, enigmatic Latin verse:

Demetrius: What's here? A scroll, and written round about?
Let's see:
[*he reads*] '*Integer vitae, scelerisque purus,*
Non eget Mauri iaculis, nec arcu.'[1]

[1] *he who leads an upright life, free from crime, has
no need of the Moor's javelins or bows*

Chiron recognises the lines from his school days, but gives them no more than a moment's thought. The words appear to be a conventional statement of the superiority of Roman virtue over barbarian violence, but Aaron realises that they have a deeper significance. The virtuous, honest man has nothing to fear, the couplet says; but Chiron and Demetrius, who possess neither virtue nor honesty, will indeed need weapons to protect themselves. Aaron congratulates Chiron on his knowledge, but is secretly contemptuous of the boys' lack of insight:

Chiron:	O, 'tis a verse in Horace;[1] I know it well:
	I read it in the grammar [2] long ago.
Aaron:	Ay, just,[3] a verse in Horace; right, you have it.
	[*aside*] Now what a thing it is to be an ass!
	Here's no sound jest.[4] The old man hath found[5] their
	guilt ...

[1] *leading Roman poet of the 1st century B.C.*
[2] *school textbook*
[3] *correct, precisely*
[4] *this is no laughing matter*
[5] *Titus has discovered*

The mood in the room is boisterous as Demetrius and Chiron, egged on by Aaron, revel in their power and freedom. Aaron mentions that he recently treated Marcus Andronicus disrespectfully, in public, despite his status as Tribune of the People; Demetrius and Chiron, for their part, boast of their violent rape of Lavinia. Their mother, who shares their deep-rooted hatred of Rome, would no doubt approve:

Aaron:	It did me good before the palace gate
	To brave[1] the tribune in his brother's hearing.
Demetrius:	But me more good to see so great a lord[2]
	Basely insinuate[3] and send us gifts.
Aaron:	Had he not reason, Lord Demetrius?
	Did you not use his daughter very friendly?
Demetrius:	I would[4] we had a thousand Roman dames
	At such a bay,[5] by turn to serve our lust.
Chiron:	A charitable wish, and full of love.
Aaron:	Here lacks but your mother[6] for to say amen.

[1] *defy, treat with contempt*
[2] *Titus*
[3] *grovel, try to ingratiate himself with us*
[4] *wish*
[5] *cornered, trapped, just as Lavinia was*
[6] *the only person missing is your mother*

At the mention of the empress, the three men are reminded that she is, as they speak, in labour. They resolve to go and pray immediately for a safe birth, but at this moment a nurse arrives: and she is carrying a newborn baby boy.

A life in the balance

The nurse is in a state of extreme distress. The birth of the empress's son is far from the joyful occasion that Rome might have expected:

Nurse:	O gentle Aaron, we are all undone.[1]
	Now help, or woe betide thee evermore!
Aaron:	Why, what a caterwauling dost thou keep!
	What dost thou wrap and fumble in thy arms?
Nurse:	O, that which I would hide from heaven's eye,
	Our empress' shame and stately Rome's disgrace.

[1] *ruined, doomed*

The reason for the nurse's agitation becomes clear when she reveals the baby to Aaron. Dark-skinned like him, the child is living proof of the empress's infidelity. Tamora has decided that ruthless action must be taken. It is unthinkable that the emperor should discover that she has been unfaithful:

Nurse:	Here is the babe, as loathsome as a toad
	Amongst the fair-faced breeders of our clime.[1]
	The empress sends it thee, thy stamp, thy seal,[2]
	And bids thee christen it with thy dagger's point.

[1] *light-skinned mothers of our region*
[2] *it has your mark on it; it is clearly yours*

Aaron responds furiously to the nurse's description of the baby. Demetrius and Chiron, meanwhile, are stunned to learn of their mother's adultery:

Aaron:	Zounds, ye whore, is black so base a hue?
	[*to the baby*] Sweet blowze,[1] you are a beauteous
	blossom, sure.
Demetrius:	Villain, what hast thou done?
Aaron:	That which thou canst not undo.

[1] *ruddy, chubby-faced little child*

As far as Demetrius and Chiron are concerned, the birth of this child is a catastrophe. They are adamant that, as their mother commanded, the boy must die. Aaron, however, is determined to let it live:

Demetrius: ... hellish dog, thou hast undone her.
Woe to her chance and damned her loathed choice,[1]
Accursed the offspring of so foul a fiend.
Chiron: It shall not live.
Aaron: It shall not die.
Nurse: Aaron, it must; the mother wills it so.

[1] *damn her misfortune and her choice of you as her lover*

For a moment, it seems that Aaron will agree to Tamora's demand; but if the baby is to be put to death, he says, he must be the one to carry out the deed. With that, he approaches the nurse, but before he can take the child from her Demetrius intervenes, determined to grab the child and kill it himself.

Aaron now draws his sword, threatening Demetrius, and seizes the baby. Anyone who harms his son in any way will be killed instantly, he warns:

Aaron: Stay, murderous villains, will you kill your brother?
Now, by the burning tapers of the sky
That shone so brightly when this boy was got,[1]
He dies upon my scimitar's sharp point
That touches this, my first-born son and heir.

[1] *the bright starlight under which he was conceived*

Shakespeare was still in his twenties when he wrote *Titus Andronicus*:

"The earliest tragedy was Titus Andronicus *... It's a young man's play full of rhetoric and violence, the Elizabethan equivalent of a Quentin Tarantino movie. No doubt those in the cheaper seats loved all the blood and guts ..."*

Michael Wood, *In Search of Shakespeare*, 2005

Whatever the empress may say, Aaron intends to keep the baby and look after it himself. The boy's dark skin is a source of pride; his colour is constant and unchangeable, unlike Demetrius and Chiron, whose complexions vary according to their emotions:

> *Aaron:*   What, what, ye sanguine,[1] shallow-hearted boys,
> Ye white-limed walls, ye alehouse painted signs![2]
> Coal-black is better than another hue
> In that it scorns to bear another hue;[3]
> For all the water in the ocean
> Can never turn the swan's black legs to white,
> Although she lave them hourly in the flood.[4]
> Tell the empress from me I am of age
> To keep mine own, excuse it how she can.[5]

> [1] *red-faced*
> [2] *whitewashed and crudely painted*
> [3] *refuses to change colour*
> [4] *washes them continually in the water*
> [5] *I am old enough to care for my child; Tamora can explain its existence however she wishes*

Demetrius and Chiron are horrified by Aaron's decision. When knowledge of the child's existence becomes public, the empress will be utterly shamed; in all probability, Saturninus will have her put to death. Aaron remains unmoved: the baby will live, come what may. Eventually the others are forced to accept his choice, but they beg Aaron to think of some way to keep themselves and the empress safe.

Still clutching the baby securely, and keeping his distance from the others, Aaron sits down. He tells the others to do the same, and an uneasy calm descends on the group. A plan of action must be agreed on, he says: they need to talk.

Keeping a secret

The first question is for the nurse. She confirms that very few people have, as yet, seen the newborn baby:

Aaron: ... how many saw the child?
Nurse: Cornelia the midwife, and myself,
And no one else but the delivered empress.

Aaron thinks for a moment. Then, without warning, he draws his scimitar and stabs the nurse, killing her instantly. The brothers jump out of their seats in shock, but Aaron remains calm, explaining that her death was necessary:

Demetrius: What mean'st thou, Aaron? Wherefore[1] didst thou this?
Aaron: O Lord, sir, 'tis a deed of policy:[2]
Shall she live to betray this guilt of ours?
A long-tongued,[3] babbling gossip? No, lords, no.

[1] *why*
[2] *expedience, pragmatism*
[3] *talkative*

It now emerges that Aaron has already formulated a plan to ensure that the emperor remains ignorant of Tamora's infidelity. He has an acquaintance, he explains, whose wife has recently given birth to a fair-skinned baby boy. Demetrius and Chiron are to visit the couple and take possession of the baby, using a combination of bribery and the promise of a bright future for the child. The infant can then be presented to the court, where there is already growing impatience for news of the empress's child:

Aaron: Go pack with him,[1] and give the mother gold,
And tell them both the circumstance of all,
And how by this[2] their child shall be advanced
And be received for[3] the emperor's heir,
And substituted in the place of mine
To calm this tempest whirling in the court;
And let the emperor dandle[4] him for his own.

[1] *come to an agreement with the husband*
[2] *in this way, by agreeing to hand over the baby*
[3] *accepted as*
[4] *dote on, pamper*

Meanwhile there is a body to dispose of, says Aaron briskly, and
he instructs the brothers to bury it in a nearby field. Then there
is the matter of dealing with the remaining witness to the birth.
She, like the nurse, must be permanently silenced:

Aaron: Hark ye, lords, you see I have given her physic,[1]
              And you must needs bestow [2] her funeral;
              The fields are near, and you are gallant grooms.[3]
              This done, see that you take no longer days,[4]
              But send the midwife presently to me.

              [1] *I have given the nurse the necessary medicine*
              [2] *provide, organise*
              [3] *fine fellows; useful assistants*
              [4] *waste no time*

Demetrius and Chiron, overawed by the Moor's ruthlessness,
assure him that he has their gratitude and loyalty:

Chiron: Aaron, I see thou wilt not trust the air
              With secrets.
Demetrius: For this care of Tamora,
              Herself and hers are highly bound to thee.

The brothers carry the body away. Now alone, Aaron considers
his next move. To keep the newborn boy safe, he decides, he
will take him to the camp of the Goths, where he will find the
friends and allies of Tamora, their captured queen. He intends
to bring the child up to be a noble fighter and leader of the Goths:

Aaron: [*to the baby*] I'll make you feed on berries and on roots,
              And fat[1] on curds and whey, and suck[2] the goat,
              And cabin[3] in a cave, and bring you up
              To be a warrior and command a camp.

              [1] *grow strong and healthy*
              [2] *drink the milk of, suckle*
              [3] *shelter, sleep*

As far as we know, there was not a single performance of Shakespeare's *Titus Andronicus* during the 18th and 19th centuries. There were several adaptations, however, in most of which the violence, harshness and moral bleakness of the original were considerably toned down.

One particularly successful adaptation was produced by the black American actor Ira Aldridge in the 1850s. Having played Othello to great acclaim in theatres throughout Europe and the United Kingdom, he later turned his attention to the role of Aaron. He commissioned a popular dramatist to revise *Titus Andronicus*, making it more acceptable to Victorian tastes as well as expanding the role of the Moor. In his advertisements, Aldridge claimed that "while the horrifying incidents have been expunged, the gems of the immortal author have been retained". However, the resulting play, though it kept the title of *Titus Andronicus*, bore little resemblance to Shakespeare's original. Aaron was transformed into an upright, honourable leader of the Goths; Tamora, his wife, was a model of respectability; and Lavinia survived unharmed to the end of the play.

A reviewer of the time was impressed by this new, sanitised version of the story:

"Titus Andronicus *is not a favourite play, and we do not know that we ever saw it produced before on any stage. A more dreadful catalogue of horrors and atrocities than it consists of would be impossible to conceive ... The* Titus Andronicus *produced under Mr Aldridge's direction is a wholly different affair; the deflowering of Lavinia, cutting out her tongue, chopping off her hands, and the numerous decapitations and gross language which occur in the original are totally omitted, and a play not only presentable but actually attractive is the result. Aaron is elevated into a noble and lofty character; Tamora, the Queen of Scythia, is a chaste though decidedly strong-minded female, and her connection with the Moor appears to be of a legitimate description; her sons Chiron and Demetrius are dutiful children, obeying the behests of their mother ...*"

Review in *The Era* weekly, 1857

A troubled mind

Driven by a burning sense of injustice, and by his hatred for the emperor Saturninus and his court, Titus is continuing to behave irrationally. He has gathered a group of relatives to help him search for Astraea, the goddess of justice who, he believes, has disappeared. Some must cast their nets in the ocean, he orders, while others are to dig until they reach the underworld.

Marcus is dismayed to see his brother in such a deluded state. Publius, Marcus's son, believes that all they can do is humour him:

Marcus:	O Publius, is not this a heavy case,[1]
	To see thy noble uncle thus distract?[2]
Publius:	Therefore, my lords, it highly us concerns
	By day and night t'attend him carefully,
	And feed his humour[3] kindly as we may
	Till time beget[4] some careful remedy.

[1] *sad state of affairs*
[2] *deranged, disturbed*
[3] *go along with his delusions*
[4] *produces, brings about*

Marcus, by contrast, fears that Titus is beyond help. The family's sole aim, he believes, must be to join Rome's old enemy and make the emperor pay for his crimes:

Marcus:	Kinsmen, his sorrows are past remedy.
	… Join with the Goths and with revengeful war
	Take wreak[1] on Rome for this ingratitude,
	And vengeance on the traitor Saturnine.

[1] *retribution*

Titus approaches Publius and asks whether he has travelled to the underworld as instructed. Publius replies that he has, but the goddess of justice was not there; Pluto, king of the underworld, believed her to be in the heavens with Jupiter. On hearing this, Titus produces a bundle of arrows with notes attached to them addressed to Jupiter, Mars, Apollo and other deities. He hands them out to his companions, ordering them all to shoot their arrows towards the heavens.

Marcus tells the group to shoot into the courtyard of the imperial palace; perhaps the attached messages will, at least, disturb the arrogant emperor.

Titus is in high spirits as he watches the volley of arrows fly upwards, convinced that his appeals for justice will attract the attention of the gods. A moment later, he spots a rustic passer-by, a country dweller carrying a pair of pigeons in a basket. This must be a messenger from the gods, he declares:

Titus: News, news from heaven! Marcus, the post[1] is come.
           Sirrah, what tidings? Have you any letters?
           Shall I have justice? What says Jupiter?

[1] *messenger*

It quickly becomes clear that the man is a simple yokel, a clown who can make no sense of Titus's baffling questions:

Titus: But what says Jupiter, I ask thee?
Clown: Alas sir, I know not Jubiter; I never drank with him
           in all my life.
Titus: Why, villain, art not thou the carrier?[1]
Clown: Ay, of my pigeons, sir, nothing else.
Titus: Why, didst thou not come from heaven?
Clown: From heaven? Alas, sir, I never came there.

[1] *carrier of Jupiter's messages*

The man explains that he is on his way to see the magistrates about a brawl between his uncle and a soldier. Titus tells him that he must instead approach the emperor himself and deliver a message. As an incentive, he offers the man money and promises to make sure that his uncle is treated fairly.

"This is a world in which people make their own laws ... the gods are frequently invoked but never reply. When the post comes with the answer to the letters which Titus shoots into the heavens, it is in the form not of a message from the gods, but of a Clown with a basket and two pigeons."

Jonathan Bate, Introduction to the Arden Shakespeare edition of *Titus Andronicus*, 2018

The man is unwilling to deliver a speech to the emperor, but agrees to hand over a letter. Titus quickly writes a note for Saturninus, then explains how the emperor should be approached. The two pigeons that the man is carrying will serve as a gift:

Titus: *[handing over the letter]* ... here is a supplication[1] for you, and when you come to him, at the first approach you must kneel, then kiss his foot, then deliver up your pigeons, and then look for your reward. I'll be at hand,[2] sir; see you do it bravely.[3]

Clown: I warrant you, sir, let me alone.[4]

[1] *a written appeal for justice*
[2] *I won't be far away*
[3] *confidently, with style*
[4] *leave it to me*

Titus then tucks a knife inside the letter, believing, in his delusionary state, that the emperor will consider it a sign of humility. Once the letter has been successfully delivered, Titus tells his new acquaintance, he is to return and describe the emperor's reaction.

The emperor lashes out   IV, iv

Saturninus is seething with anger. He has found Titus's letters, attached to arrows and shot into the palace grounds, and is furious at their contents. Titus's claim that justice has not been done is outrageous, he tells his attendants:

Saturninus: Was ever seen
An emperor in Rome thus overborne,[1]
Troubled, confronted thus, and for the extent
Of equal justice used in such contempt?[2]

[1] *oppressed, insulted*
[2] *treated with such disrespect in return for exercising justice impartially*

In his messages, addressed to the gods, Titus claims that his sons Quintus and Martius were put to death unjustly by the emperor. Saturninus, stung by this accusation, insists that their execution was entirely legal, as they were found guilty of the murder of his brother Bassianus:

> *Saturninus:* My lords, you know, as know the mightful[1] gods,
> However these disturbers of our peace
> Buzz in the people's ears,[2] there nought hath passed
> But even with law[3] against the wilful sons
> Of old Andronicus.

> [1] *mighty*
> [2] *try to spread rumours*
> [3] *everything was done in complete accordance with the law*

Titus may well have been devastated by the loss of his sons, Saturninus admits, and he is certainly behaving strangely: but that does not give him the right to harass the emperor or spread lies about Roman justice. Besides, his apparent insanity is probably a pretence, and will not allow him to escape the law. The punishment for conspiring against the emperor can be extremely severe:

> *Saturninus:*   … if I live, his feigned ecstasies[1]
> Shall be no shelter to these outrages,[2]
> But he and his shall know that justice lives
> In Saturninus' health,[3] whom, if she sleep,
> He'll so awake as she in fury shall
> Cut off the proud'st conspirator that lives.[4]

> [1] *simulated bouts of madness*
> [2] *will not provide an excuse for his crimes*
> [3] *Titus and his family must realise that justice will endure as long as I am alive*
> [4] *if justice sleeps, I'll rouse her so forcefully that she will destroy every last conspirator in her fury*

Tamora makes a show of trying to pacify her husband. Titus is old, she pleads, and heartbroken by his sons' death; he should be comforted rather than punished. She knows, however, that her words will have no effect on the emperor, and that Titus's fate is sealed. She relishes the prospect of his execution, which will finally bring revenge for the slaughter of her son Alarbus.

The rustic simpleton sent by Titus now enters, and presents his letter to the emperor as instructed. His greeting is respectful, but Saturninus, already ill-tempered, is enraged even further to discover that the man brings yet another message from the deceitful old general. To make matters worse, a knife has been hidden inside the scroll. This messenger is clearly an accomplice in Titus's treacherous plans, and must be dealt with swiftly and ruthlessly:

Tamora:	How now, good fellow, wouldst thou speak with us?
Clown:	Yea, forsooth, an your mistress-ship be emperial.[1]
Tamora:	Empress I am, but yonder sits the emperor.
Clown:	'Tis he. God and Saint Stephen give you good e'en.[2]
	I have brought you a letter and a couple of pigeons here.
	[*Saturninus reads the letter*]
Saturninus:	Go, take him away and hang him presently!

[1] *if your ladyship is a ruler of the empire*
[2] *evening, afternoon*

The innocent clown, confused and still expecting his reward, is dragged away to his death.

Saturninus, incensed at Titus's continual appeals for justice, announces that he has lost patience. He orders his attendants to seize the general and bring him to the imperial palace:

Saturninus: May this be borne[1] as if his traitorous sons,
That died by law for murder of our brother,
Have by my means[2] been butchered wrongfully?
Go, drag the villain hither by the hair:
Nor age nor honour shall shape privilege.[3]

[1] *tolerated*
[2] *because of me, with my consent*
[3] *neither his age nor his status will give him immunity from prosecution*

Saturninus now makes no secret of the fact that he wants Titus dead; his attempt to employ a clown to deliver his latest message is the last straw. The general had supported him in his bid to become emperor, but it is now clear to Saturninus that Titus had always intended to overthrow him and gain the crown for himself:

Saturninus:	For this proud mock I'll be thy slaughterman,
	Sly frantic wretch that holp'st to make me great [1]
	In hope thyself should govern Rome and me.

[1] *helped me to become emperor*

A new crisis

Before Saturninus's order can be carried out, Emillius, the emperor's trusted messenger, rushes into the imperial palace. He brings devastating news: the Goths, despite their recent defeat, have regrouped, and are advancing on Rome at this very moment. The army is commanded not by a Goth but by a Roman, none other than Titus's eldest son Lucius:

Emillius:	Arm, arm, my lords! Rome never had more cause:
	The Goths have gathered head,[1] and with a power
	Of high-resolved men bent to the spoil [2]
	They hither march amain [3] under conduct [4]
	Of Lucius, son to old Andronicus ...

[1] *raised an army*
[2] *with a force of determined men intent on destruction*
[3] *at full tilt*
[4] *leadership*

The news comes as a crushing blow to Saturninus. He fears Lucius, whom he himself banished for attempting to rescue his condemned brothers. Saturninus has, on occasions, wandered around the city in disguise, and he knows that there is great sympathy and support for Lucius among the citizens of Rome. The empress tries, without success, to offer reassurance:

Tamora:	Why should you fear? Is not your city strong?
Saturninus:	Ay, but the citizens favour Lucius
	And will revolt from me to succour him.
Tamora:	King, be thy thoughts imperious like thy name.[1]
	Is the sun dimmed, that gnats do fly in it?
	The eagle suffers [2] little birds to sing,
	And is not careful [3] what they mean thereby ...

[1] *Saturn was a king who presided over the mythical Golden Age of Rome*
[2] *allows*
[3] *does not care, takes no notice*

Tamora does not share her husband's pessimism. She believes that Titus is the one man who can dissuade his son from attacking Rome; and she is confident that, given the opportunity, she will be able to bring the old general under her control:

> *Tamora:*   ... know thou, emperor,
> I will enchant the old Andronicus
> With words more sweet and yet more dangerous
> Than baits to fish, or honey-stalks[1] to sheep,
> When as the one is wounded with the bait,
> The other rotted with delicious feed.

> [1] *clover flowers, attractive and palatable to sheep,*
> *but believed to cause bloating and eventually death*
> *if eaten to excess*

The empress, aware of her husband's hesitancy, decides to take action. She orders the messenger Emillius to travel to the Goths' camp and ask Lucius to attend negotiations with the emperor in Rome. The talks will be held at the Andronicus family home.

Saturninus gives his approval to the plan, and Emillius sets off at once. Tamora assures her husband that, in the meantime, she will persuade Titus to act in the interests of Rome:

> *Tamora:*   Now will I to that old Andronicus,
> And temper[1] him with all the art I have
> To pluck proud Lucius from the warlike Goths.
> And now, sweet emperor, be blithe[2] again
> And bury all thy fear in my devices.[3]

> [1] *work on, influence*
> [2] *carefree, cheerful*
> [3] *don't be afraid; my plans will take care of everything*

An old enemy   V, i

The Goths' military camp is a scene of noisy, purposeful activity as the troops prepare for an assault on Rome. A fanfare of trumpets and the beating of drums herald the entrance of their leader Lucius, who has encouraging news. The people of Rome, impatient to be free of the tyrannical Saturninus, have assured him that they are ready to welcome him into the city:

Lucius: Approved warriors and my faithful friends,
I have received letters from great Rome
Which signifies what hate they bear their emperor,
And how desirous of our sight[1] they are.
Therefore, great lords, be as your titles witness,[2]
Imperious, and impatient of your wrongs;
And wherein Rome hath done you any scath,
Let him make treble satisfaction.[3]

[1] *the arrival of Lucius and his army*
[2] *be noble, like the titles that have been bestowed
on you*
[3] *make Rome pay three times over for any wrongs it
has committed against you*

**The Goths declare their loyalty to their new leader, knowing that
he has turned against his ungrateful homeland:**

Goth: Brave slip[1] sprung from the great Andronicus,
Whose name was once our terror, now our comfort,
Whose high exploits and honourable deeds
Ingrateful Rome requites[2] with foul contempt,
Be bold[3] in us. We'll follow where thou lead'st ...

[1] *offspring*
[2] *rewards*
[3] *confident, trustful*

**Lucius's attention is suddenly caught by the sight of a stranger
being brought into the camp. The man, a Moor, is carrying a
young child. Lucius immediately recognises him as Aaron,
Tamora's attendant, who tricked Titus into sacrificing his own
hand in the false hope that his sons would be spared. The child,
he assumes, is Tamora's:**

Lucius: ... this is the incarnate[1] devil
That robbed Andronicus of his good hand;
This is the pearl that pleased your empress' eye,
And here's the base fruit of her burning lust.

[1] *personified, embodied*

Without hesitation, Lucius orders the execution of Aaron and his child. A ladder is placed against a tree, and the Moor is forced to climb up it in preparation for his hanging. Aaron calls on Lucius to spare his son, whose mother was queen of the Goths:

Lucius: A halter,[1] soldiers! Hang him on this tree,
And by his side his fruit of bastardy.
Aaron: Touch not the boy, he is of royal blood.
Lucius: Too like the sire for ever being good.[2]

[1] *rope, noose*
[2] *he is too similar to his father ever to have any good qualities*

Aaron repeats his plea for the boy's life. In return, he promises, he will reveal everything he knows about the devastating events that have afflicted the Andronicus family. Lucius cautiously agrees, but Aaron warns him that he will find the truth almost unbearable:

Lucius: Say on, and if it please me which thou speak'st,
Thy child shall live and I will see it nourished.
Aaron: And if it please thee? Why, assure thee, Lucius,
'Twill vex thy soul to hear what I shall speak:
For I must talk of murders, rapes and massacres,
Acts of black night, abominable deeds ...
... And this shall all be buried in my death
Unless thou swear to me my child shall live.

An unrepentant sinner

Lucius gives his word that, whatever horrors Aaron may disclose, the boy will be spared. Aaron insists, however, that Lucius must swear a formal, religious oath. He is scornful of religion himself, he says dismissively, but accepts that it means a great deal to its adherents. Eventually Lucius agrees:

Aaron: ... I urge[1] thy oath; for that[2] I know
An idiot holds his bauble[3] for a god
And keeps the oath which by that god he swears,
To that I'll urge him; therefore thou shalt vow
By that same god, what god soe'er it be
That thou adorest and hast in reverence,

	To save my boy, to nourish and bring him up,
	Or else I will discover[4] nought to thee.
Lucius:	Even by my god I swear to thee I will.

[1] *demand, insist on*
[2] *because, since*
[3] *jester's stick, topped with a comical carved head*
[4] *disclose, reveal*

Lucius listens in revulsion as Aaron, high up on the ladder and clearly relishing his position of power, tells him that the empress's sons are guilty of murder, rape and mutilation. He was the one behind the attack, he claims proudly:

Aaron:	'Twas her[1] two sons that murdered Bassianus;
	They cut thy sister's tongue and ravished her,
	And cut her hands and trimmed[2] her as thou sawest.
Lucius:	O detestable villain! Call'st thou that trimming?
Aaron:	Why, she was washed and cut and trimmed,
	And 'twas trim[3] sport for them which had the doing
	of it.
Lucius:	O barbarous, beastly villains like thyself!
Aaron:	Indeed, I was their tutor to instruct them.

[1] *Tamora's*
[2] *cut up neatly; prepared, like a piece of meat*
[3] *fine*

It was he, boasts Aaron, who dug the pit into which Bassianus's body was thrown; he too hid the gold and forged the letter which incriminated Titus's innocent sons. He recalls how he tricked Titus into losing his hand, and secretly watched his reaction as he was presented with the heads of his executed sons:

Aaron:	I played the cheater[1] for thy father's hand
	And when I had it, drew myself apart
	And almost broke my heart with extreme laughter.
	I pried me[2] through the crevice of a wall
	When, for[3] his hand, he had his two sons' heads,
	Beheld his tears and laughed so heartily
	That both mine eyes were rainy like to his …

[1] *played a trick*
[2] *peered, spied*
[3] *in return for*

In the early 1590s, Shakespeare's literary career was just beginning. He had had some success both as an actor and as a playwright, particularly with his dramatic renderings of the reigns of Henry VI and Richard III; life in the theatre, however, was extremely precarious. London's playhouses were frequently shut down due to plague, and acting companies – which needed the sponsorship of wealthy, influential individuals – were continually breaking up and reforming.

At this time, Shakespeare was also pursuing a career as a poet. With the patronage of the Earl of Southampton, a charismatic young aristocrat, he published two long poems on mythological themes, *Venus and Adonis* and *The Rape of Lucrece*, both of which were well received and reprinted several times.

The year 1594 seems to have been pivotal for the thirty-year-old Shakespeare. The plague subsided; the theatres reopened after a two-year hiatus; and Shakespeare joined a group of actors who would go on to become London's most successful, stable and long-lasting theatre company. Perhaps the success of *Titus Andronicus*, performed for the first time in 1594, influenced Shakespeare's decision to pursue a career in the theatre rather than poetry?

"At that time, he was torn between pursuing a career in the theatre and one in which he sought advancement by securing aristocratic patronage through his published poetry. For a while he had done both, but the rewards of patronage either didn't materialize or proved unsatisfying. Theatre won out ... After joining the Chamberlain's Men in 1594, Shakespeare hit his stride in the next two years with a great burst of innovative plays: A Midsummer Night's Dream, Love's Labour's Lost, Romeo and Juliet, King John, Richard the Second, The Merchant of Venice *and* The First Part of Henry the Fourth. *"*

James Shapiro, *1599: A Year in the Life of William Shakespeare*, 2005

Lucius asks, in horrified amazement, whether Aaron now repents his crimes. Despite the fact that he is about to be hanged, Aaron remains defiant. He has done countless evil deeds during his life, and regrets none of them:

Lucius:	Art thou not sorry for these heinous deeds?
Aaron:	Ay, that I had not done a thousand more.
	Even now I curse the day – and yet I think
	Few come within the compass of my curse [1] –
	Wherein I did not some notorious ill,
	As [2] kill a man or else devise his death,
	Ravish a maid or plot the way to do it,
	Accuse some innocent and forswear myself, [3]
	Set deadly enmity between two friends …

[1] *there were few days which were like this*
[2] *such as*
[3] *swear falsely*

Lucius, appalled at this catalogue of wickedness, decides that Aaron must not be hanged; he intends to devise a more agonising death for the Moor. He orders his followers to take Aaron down from the ladder, and to gag him so that he can no longer brag about his lifelong crime spree.

At this point Emillius, the emperor's messenger, arrives. He has been sent, he announces, to request a truce: the emperor wishes to meet Lucius for peace talks, to take place at his father's house in Rome. Lucius gives his consent. The advance on Rome is halted and, for the time being, the city is safe.

Unearthly visitors V, ii

Tamora has devised a plan to gather the Andronicus family under one roof. When they are together she will be able, finally, to take vengeance for the death of her eldest son Alarbus. She can never forget how Lucius demanded his execution, hacking him to pieces and burning his limbs in a sacrificial fire; nor how her desperate pleas for mercy, made to Titus as she knelt before him, were rejected.

It is clear to Tamora that Titus, who has been behaving strangely for some time, has by now lost his grip on reality. Aware that he has become obsessed with punishing his enemies, she has come to Titus's house disguised as the goddess of Revenge, wearing a dark, sombre costume. She intends to offer Titus her help, as a deity, in achieving his objectives:

Tamora: Thus, in this strange and sad habiliment,[1]
I will encounter with Andronicus
And say I am Revenge, sent from below [2]
To join with him and right his heinous wrongs;
Knock at his study, where they say he keeps [3]
To ruminate strange plots of dire revenge;
Tell him Revenge is come to join with him
And work confusion [4] on his enemies.

[1] *dark, dismal clothing*
[2] *the underworld*
[3] *remains, lies in wait*
[4] *bring about destruction*

Tamora knocks at the door, and Titus appears at a balcony above her. At first he claims to recognise her, and is reluctant to let her in, fearing that she will cause him even more injury. She persuades him that she is a visitor from the underworld, and has come to assist him:

Titus: ... I know thee well
For our proud empress, mighty Tamora.
Is not thy coming for my other hand?
Tamora: Know, thou sad man, I am not Tamora;
She is thy enemy and I thy friend.
I am Revenge, sent from th'infernal kingdom
To ease the gnawing vulture of thy mind [1]
By working wreakful [2] vengeance on thy foes.
Come down and welcome me to this world's light ...

[1] *in Greek mythology, Prometheus was tormented by an eagle that gnawed continually at his liver; the organ was regenerated every night, so his agony was never-ending*
[2] *merciless, implacable*

Tamora's sons are with her, disguised as the personifications of Rape and Murder. Again, Titus feels that he recognises them, but Tamora contradicts him; they are her agents of revenge, she explains, tasked with tracking down murderers and rapists. Titus eventually agrees to let the three otherworldly visitors into his house:

Tamora:	These are my ministers, and come with me.
Titus:	Are these thy ministers? What are they called?
Tamora:	Rape and Murder, therefore called so
	'Cause they take vengeance of such kind of men.
Titus:	Good Lord, how like the empress' sons they are,
	And you the empress! But we worldly men
	Have miserable, mad, mistaking eyes.
	O sweet Revenge, now do I come to thee,
	And if one arm's embracement will content thee,
	I will embrace thee in it by and by.

Plotting revenge

As Titus makes his way downstairs, Tamora, pleased with the success of her ruse, tells Demetrius and Chiron to follow her lead and humour the general's madness. She will persuade him to invite his son Lucius to a banquet, she tells them. As leader of the Goths, Lucius will be attended by guards; she is confident that she will be able to distract them, leaving Lucius vulnerable to attack.

Titus now comes to the door and greets the visitors warmly, remarking yet again how similar they are to Tamora and her sons:

Titus:	Long have I been forlorn, and all for thee.[1]
	Welcome, dread Fury,[2] to my woeful house;
	Rapine and Murder, you are welcome too.
	How like the empress and her sons you are!

[1] *for the lack of revenge*
[2] *avenging goddess of Greek mythology*

Tamora asks how she and her ministers can be of service to Titus. In response, he speaks to the figure of Murder, and asks him to hunt down and kill Demetrius; he then turns to Rape, instructing him to kill Chiron. Finally he addresses Revenge herself, asking her to deal with the empress and her attendant:

> Titus: [*to Tamora*] Go thou with them, and in the emperor's
> court
> There is a queen attended by a Moor –
> Well shalt thou know her by thine own proportion,[1]
> For up and down[2] she doth resemble thee –
> I pray thee, do on them some violent death:
> They have been violent to me and mine.[3]
>
> Tamora: Well hast thou lessened us; this shall we do.

> [1] *you will recognise her by her similarity to you*
> [2] *from head to toe*
> [3] *my family*

Tamora, in the guise of Revenge, promises to comply with Titus's request. However, she proposes a different way in which his enemies can be crushed. If he invites them to a banquet, she will ensure that they all attend, and are all at his mercy: he can then take his longed-for revenge. The banquet could be held under the pretext of peace talks with Lucius, who is now threatening Rome at the head of an advancing army:

> Tamora: But would it please thee, good Andronicus,
> To send for Lucius, thy thrice-valiant son,
> Who leads towards Rome a band of warlike Goths,
> And bid him come and banquet at thy house?
> When he is here, even at thy solemn feast,
> I will bring in the empress and her sons,
> The emperor himself and all thy foes,
> And at thy mercy shall they stoop and kneel,
> And on them shalt thou ease thy angry heart.[1]

> [1] *deal with them as you wish; relieve your suffering*
> *by taking revenge on them*

Titus agrees. He calls out for his brother Marcus, and instructs him to arrange the banquet without delay. Marcus sets off to the Goths' camp at once, to ask Lucius to halt his advance and to come to his father's house to negotiate peace with Rome.

The three visitors are about to leave, but Titus insists that Revenge's two attendants, Rape and Murder, stay behind. Tamora takes her sons aside and reminds them, again, to play along with the general's eccentric behaviour. In the meantime, she will return to her husband to report that her subterfuge has been successful. The Andronicus clan will all be gathered at the banquet, ripe for slaughter:

Tamora: [*aside, to her sons*] What say you, boys, will you abide
        with him
        Whiles I go tell my lord the emperor
        How I have governed our determined jest?[1]
        Yield to his humour, smooth and speak him fair,[2]
        And tarry with him till I turn again.[3]

        [1] *how I have carried out our planned deception*
        [2] *flatter Titus, and indulge him*
        [3] *return*

As Tamora speaks to her sons, Titus reveals that he knows perfectly well who the visitors are. He is feigning gullibility, and in reality it is he who is humouring them. When the disguised figure of Revenge takes her leave, he bids her a fond farewell. Her promise that he will have his vengeance is truer than she realises:

Titus: [*aside*] I know them all, though they suppose me mad,
        And will o'erreach them in their own devices:[1]
        A pair of cursed hell-hounds and their dam!
Demetrius: Madam, depart at pleasure, leave us here.
Tamora: Farewell, Andronicus; Revenge now goes
        To lay a complot to betray thy foes.[2]
Titus: I know thou dost; and sweet Revenge, farewell.

        [1] *beat them at their own game*
        [2] *to prepare a plot that will trap your enemies*

The death toll rises

Demetrius and Chiron are now alone with Titus. They believe
that the old general, in his deranged state, has been deceived
by their disguises; but their confidence is shattered when Titus
calls for three of his kinsmen, ordering them to seize the young
men and tie them up.

Titus suggests, sarcastically, that they are indeed visitors from
the underworld. As murderers and rapists, however, their crimes
are real, and Titus finally has his opportunity for revenge:

Titus:	Know you these two?
Publius:	The empress' sons I take them:[1] Chiron, Demetrius.
Titus:	Fie,[2] Publius, fie, thou art too much deceived.
	The one is Murder, and Rape is the other's name,
	And therefore bind them, gentle Publius;
	Caius and Valentine, lay hands on them.
	Oft you have heard me wish for such an hour,
	And now I find it; therefore bind them sure,
	And stop their mouths if they begin to cry.

[1] *recognise them, believe them to be*
[2] *shame on you*

Titus leaves for a moment as Demetrius and Chiron are bound
and gagged by his three kinsmen. When he returns, he is
carrying a knife. His daughter Lavinia is with him, holding a large
basin in her mutilated arms. Tamora's sons, unable to speak or
move, are forced to listen as Titus recites their crimes:

Titus:	O villains, Chiron and Demetrius,
	Here stands the spring[1] whom you have stained with mud,
	This goodly summer with your winter mixed.
	You killed her husband, and for that vile fault
	Two of her brothers were condemned to death,
	My hand cut off and made a merry jest,
	Both her sweet hands, her tongue, and that more dear
	Than hands or tongue, her spotless chastity,
	Inhuman traitors, you constrained and forced.[2]

[1] *fount of purity; Lavinia*
[2] *took forcibly, raped*

Titus now describes to his terrified victims the gruesome nature of his planned revenge:

Titus: Hark, wretches, how I mean to martyr you: [1]
           This one hand yet is left to cut your throats,
           Whiles that Lavinia 'tween her stumps doth hold
           The basin that receives your guilty blood.

[1] *kill you violently*

The killings that take place in *Titus Andronicus* are motivated by a number of different factors. Revenge is the principal motivation, but other motives include religious observance (as in the killing of Alarbus); simple expediency (as in the killing of the nurse who witnessed the birth of Tamora's child); the command of an emperor (which led to the death of the clown); and the judgement of a court of law (the claim made for the execution of Titus's sons Martius and Quintus). The distinction between lawful and unlawful killing, as well as the concept of justice itself, is far from clear in the world of *Titus Andronicus*.

The ritual nature of the killing of Chiron and Demetrius might well put an Elizabethan audience in mind of a public execution. The most severe penalty inflicted by the state – hanging, drawing and quartering – was a gruesome theatrical spectacle with more than a hint of revenge about it. For example, the sentence handed down to the Duke of Buckingham, convicted of treason in 1521, was worded as follows:

"You are to be laid on a hurdle and drawn [1] to the place of execution, and there to be hanged, cut down alive, your members [2] to be cut off and cast in the fire, your bowels burnt before you, your head smitten off, and your body quartered and divided at the King's will, and God have mercy on your soul."

[1] *tied to a wooden frame and dragged*
[2] *genitals*

Three such executions, attended by large crowds, took place in London in 1594, the year when *Titus Andronicus* first appeared on stage. One of the victims was Roderigo Lopes, Queen Elizabeth's own physician, accused of conspiring to poison the Queen.

Tamora too must be made to suffer, declares Titus. He has devised a horrific form of vengeance, to take place under cover of the planned banquet:

> *Titus:* You know your mother means to feast with me,
> And calls herself Revenge, and thinks me mad.
> Hark, villains, I will grind your bones to dust,
> And with your blood and it I'll make a paste,[1]
> And of the paste a coffin I will rear,[2]
> And make two pasties[3] of your shameful heads,
> And bid that strumpet, your unhallowed dam,
> Like to the earth swallow her own increase.[4]
> This is the feast that I have bid her to,
> And this the banquet she shall surfeit on[5] ...

> [1] *dough*
> [2] *create a large pastry crust*
> [3] *meat pies*
> [4] *consume her own offspring, like the earth receiving its dead*
> [5] *feast on, eat to excess*

Without further ado, Titus swiftly cuts the two brothers' throats. Lavinia, for her part, willingly collects the blood of the men who raped her and murdered her husband. The bodies are unceremoniously dragged away to be hacked to pieces and cooked. Every last morsel will be fed to Tamora and the other unsuspecting guests at the approaching feast.

An uneasy truce   V, iii

Titus's son Lucius has been threatening to invade Rome, with the support of the Goths, and to depose the unpopular emperor Saturninus. However, at the request of his father, who has sent Marcus as his messenger, Lucius has agreed to call a temporary halt to his advance on Rome. He has now come to Titus's house to attend a banquet and hold peace talks with the emperor.

Lucius is accompanied by a group of Goths. Also with him is the prisoner Aaron, already under sentence of death. While the banquet takes place, Lucius tells Marcus, the Moor must be securely shackled. Later, he may prove valuable as an informer against the empress:

Lucius:	Good uncle, take you in this barbarous Moor,
	This ravenous tiger, this accursed devil;
	Let him receive no sustenance, fetter him
	Till he be brought unto the empress' face
	For testimony of her foul proceedings.[1]

> [1] *brought into Tamora's presence to give evidence of her wicked activities*

As he enters the house, Lucius mentions that he is extremely distrustful of Saturninus. Although they are supposedly meeting for a peace conference, Lucius suspects that the emperor intends to take this opportunity to get rid of his opponent. He asks Marcus to ensure that there are enough armed men lying in wait to deal with any possible attack:

Lucius:	… see the ambush of our friends be strong:[1]
	I fear the emperor means no good to us.

> [1] *make sure that we have plenty of hidden guards who are ready to react quickly*

At this moment the blare of trumpets heralds the arrival of the emperor himself, accompanied by the empress, noblemen and attendants. The initial exchange between Saturninus and his rival is inauspicious as the emperor implies that he alone is the legitimate leader of Rome. Marcus urges the two men to remain calm and negotiate respectfully:

Saturninus:	What, hath the firmament more suns than one?[1]
Lucius:	What boots it thee[2] to call thyself a sun?
Marcus:	Rome's emperor, and nephew, break the parle;[3]
	These quarrels must be quietly debated.
	The feast is ready which the careful[4] Titus
	Hath ordained to an honourable end,
	For peace, for love, for league[5] and good to Rome.
	Please you, therefore, draw nigh and take your places.
Saturninus:	Marcus, we will.

> [1] *is there more than one sun in the sky?*
> [2] *what good does it do*
> [3] *begin the parley; open the negotiations*
> [4] *sorrowful, careworn*
> [5] *unity, fellowship*

A banqueting table is brought in, and the assembled company take their seats. It is a sizeable gathering: around the table are the emperor and his wife; the Roman courtiers and senators; Lucius and his attendant guards from the army of the Goths; and members of the Andronicus family.

Titus himself now enters, and starts placing dishes on the table. To the surprise of his guests, he is dressed not as a general but as a cook. He welcomes everyone to the feast, and urges them to start eating:

Titus: Welcome, my gracious lord; welcome, dread[1] queen;
            Welcome, ye warlike Goths; welcome, Lucius;
            And welcome all. Although the cheer[2] be poor,
            'Twill fill your stomachs. Please you, eat of it.

            [1] *mighty, awe-inspiring*
            [2] *fare, food*

The banquet begins.

"In Titus Andronicus, *Shakespeare takes the revenge play beyond the norm. In the usual revenge play, we know who the bad guys are: they have killed and they keep killing – they must be stopped, paid back, made sorry. And they are. It is one wild ride of unambiguous identification for the audience ... At the end we are strangely satisfied by revenge's strange 'moral'. Not so with* Titus. *It has two wild rides back to back. This twinning or mirroring radically changes our sense of revenge itself to something unsatisfying and immoral, for while we identify with each avenger in turn, we see the whole more clearly."*

Dr Susan Willis, *Shakespeare's Double Helix*, 2007

A deadly settlement

As the guests eat, Titus poses a question to Saturninus. It concerns the story of a Roman military officer, Virginius, who killed his own daughter to release her from the shame of having been raped. This was the virtuous, honourable thing to do, states the emperor:

Titus: My lord the emperor, resolve me this:
             Was it well done of rash Virginius
             To slay his daughter with his own right hand,
             Because she was enforced, stained and deflowered?
Saturninus: It was, Andronicus.
Titus: Your reason, mighty lord?
Saturninus: Because the girl should not survive her shame,
             And by her presence still renew his sorrows.[1]

> [1] *be a continual source of sadness to him*

Titus accepts the emperor's verdict and praises his judgement. He then turns to the shrouded, silent figure next to him: pulling off her veil, he reveals the mutilated Lavinia, her tongue cut out and her hands hacked away. His next act leaves his guests appalled and bewildered:

Titus: A reason mighty, strong, and effectual;
             A pattern, precedent, and lively warrant [1]
             For me, most wretched, to perform the like.[2]
             [*he unveils Lavinia*]
             Die, die, Lavinia, and thy shame with thee,
             And with thy shame thy father's sorrow die.
             [*he kills Lavinia*]
Saturninus: What hast thou done, unnatural and unkind?

> [1] *striking example*
> [2] *to do the same*

Titus, beside himself with grief and anger, declares that he has done the right thing, just like Virginius in the story. Despite the shock and uproar that he has just created, he insists that the emperor and his wife continue to eat. Eventually he names Lavinia's assailants:

Titus: I am as woeful as Virginius was,
                     And have a thousand times more cause than he
                     To do this outrage; and it now is done.
Saturninus: What, was she ravished? Tell who did the deed.
Titus: Will't please you eat? Will't please your highness feed?
Tamora: Why hast thou slain thine only daughter thus?
Titus: Not I, 'twas Chiron and Demetrius:
                     They ravished her and cut away her tongue,
                     And they, 'twas they, that did her all this wrong.

The emperor calls out for the two young men to be brought before him immediately. Titus replies that they are already present:

Saturninus: Go, fetch them hither to us presently.
Titus: Why, there they are, both baked in this pie,
                     Whereof their mother daintily hath fed,
                     Eating the flesh that she herself hath bred.

... there they are, both baked in this pie,
Whereof their mother daintily hath fed,
Eating the flesh that she herself hath bred.

In this final blood-soaked scene, the brutal confrontation is accompanied, bizarrely, by a series of rhyming couplets:

"Beneath the violence there is a scarcely concealed pantomime absurdity that leaves its mark in the inevitable tick-tock of its rhymes."

Bart Van Es, *Shakespeare in Company*, 2013

Titus shows them the very knife with which he cut his victims' throats: and before Tamora has time to react, he plunges it into her breast, killing her instantly. The banquet descends into tumult and confusion as Saturninus stabs Titus in retaliation: and Lucius, in response, kills the emperor.

Fighting breaks out between the emperor's guards and the Goths, scattering the guests, and amid the screams and chaos Lucius and Marcus escape to an upper balcony.

Appealing to the crowd

Speaking from the balcony, protected by armed Goths, Marcus addresses the assembly below. The scene is one of carnage and disorder: the lifeless bodies of the emperor and his wife, and of Titus and his daughter, are all lying where they have fallen. As Tribune of the People, Marcus calls for the restoration of order and unity:

> *Marcus:* You sad-faced men, people and sons of Rome,
> By uproars severed,[1] as a flight of fowl
> Scattered by winds and high tempestuous gusts,
> O let me teach you how to knit again
> This scattered corn into one mutual[2] sheaf,
> These broken limbs again into one body.
>
> [1] *torn apart by upheavals*
> [2] *cohesive, self-supporting*

A guest at the banquet cries out, in despair, that Rome is beyond help. Its emperor has been murdered, and his killer, a Roman, appears to have led an invading army of Goths into the heart of the city:

> *Roman Lord:* Let Rome herself be bane[1] unto herself,
> And she whom mighty kingdoms curtsy to,
> Like a forlorn[2] and desperate castaway,
> Do shameful execution on herself!
>
> [1] *poison; destroyer*
> [2] *abandoned*

Marcus is anxious to explain the suffering that the Andronicus clan has gone through, and to justify the killing of Saturninus. He is overcome with emotion, however, and calls on Lucius to speak to the gathering.

Lucius recounts the terrible events leading up to the catastrophe that they have just witnessed: the murder of the emperor's brother Bassianus, the rape and mutilation of Lavinia, the wrongful execution of Titus's sons, and the deceitful sacrifice of Titus's hand. He himself was banished, Lucius tells the guests, for trying to save his brothers' lives. However, he never lost his love for Rome, he vows, even though he sought help from the empire's old enemy, the Goths. He has fought for Rome many times, alongside his father, as his scars prove:

Lucius: I am the turned-forth,[1] be it known to you,
That have preserved her welfare[2] in my blood,
And from her bosom took the enemy's point,
Sheathing the steel in my adventurous body.[3]
Alas, you know I am no vaunter,[4] I;
My scars can witness, dumb although they are,
That my report is just and full of truth.

[1] *outcast, exile*
[2] *kept the well-being of Rome alive*
[3] *removed the enemy's sword that was threatening Rome, and took the blows myself, putting my own body at risk*
[4] *boaster, braggart*

Marcus, regaining his composure, now intervenes. He points to a baby in the arms of one of Lucius's guards: this is the empress's illegitimate child, he tells the onlookers. His father Aaron, who was at the root of the disasters that befell the Andronicus family, is now in captivity, and will confirm everything that Lucius has alleged. Marcus asks his audience to consider whether Titus was justified in wanting revenge for the wrongs done to him and his family:

Marcus: Behold the child:
Of this was Tamora delivered,
The issue of an irreligious Moor,
Chief architect and plotter of these woes.

The villain is alive in Titus' house,
And as he is to witness this is true,
Now judge what cause had Titus to revenge
These wrongs unspeakable, past patience,[1]
Or more than any living man could bear.

[1] *beyond endurance, intolerable*

Marcus now makes a dramatic gesture. Standing with Lucius at the very edge of the balcony, he asks those present to judge whether they are guilty of wrongdoing. If so, he declares, they will throw themselves down to the stone floor below, bringing the entire house of Andronicus to an end:

Marcus: Now have you heard the truth: what say you, Romans?
Have we done aught amiss, show us wherein,[1]
And from the place where you behold us pleading,
The poor remainder of Andronici
Will, hand in hand, all headlong hurl ourselves,
And on the ragged[2] stones beat forth our souls,
And make a mutual closure of our house.[3]
Speak, Romans, speak ...

[1] *if we have done anything unjust, tell us what it is*
[2] *rugged, rough*
[3] *together bring our family line to an end*

... hand in hand, all headlong hurl ourselves ...

The word 'hand' is used more frequently in *Titus Andronicus* than in any other play by Shakespeare:

"In a play pre-eminently concerned with the mutilation of the human body, Titus Andronicus *makes nearly sixty references, figurative as well as literal, to the word 'hand' and eighteen more to the word 'head' ... the figurative language points continually toward the lurid events that govern the tragedy."*

Albert H. Tricomi, *The Aesthetics of Mutilation*, 1974

A last kiss

The nobleman Emillius, the dead emperor's trusted attendant, is the first to speak. Marcus is held in high regard as tribune, and Lucius, popular with the Roman people, is the clear choice to succeed Saturninus:

Emillius: [*to Marcus*] Come, come, thou reverend man of Rome,
              And bring our emperor gently in thy hand,
              Lucius, our emperor, for well I know
              The common voice do cry it shall be so.
Marcus: Lucius, all hail, Rome's royal emperor!

Amidst enthusiastic cheering and shouting, Marcus and Lucius descend from the balcony into the banqueting hall. Lucius addresses the Romans, vowing to restore the well-being of Rome now that the reign of the hated Saturninus is over. First, however, he must pay his respects to his father, whose lifeless body is still lying where it fell. He calls on Marcus to join him:

Romans: Lucius, all hail, Rome's gracious governor!
Lucius: Thanks, gentle Romans. May I govern so
            To heal Rome's harms and wipe away her woe.
            But, gentle people, give me aim[1] awhile,
            For nature puts me to a heavy task.
            Stand all aloof,[2] but, uncle, draw you near
            To shed obsequious[3] tears upon this trunk.

[1] *stand by; wait and observe*
[2] *aside*
[3] *dutiful, appropriate to a funeral*

Lucius kisses Titus sorrowfully, and Marcus does the same. Lucius's son is with them, and they remind him of the old man's love for his grandson:

Lucius: [*to his son*] Thy grandsire loved thee well:
            Many a time he danced thee on his knee,
            Sung thee asleep, his loving breast thy pillow;
            Many a story hath he told to thee,
            And bid thee bear his pretty tales in mind
            And talk of them when he was dead and gone.

Marcus: How many thousand times hath these poor lips,
            When they were living, warmed themselves on thine!

The boy gives his grandfather a final kiss, but can hardly bring
himself to say farewell:

Young Lucius: [*kisses Titus*] O grandsire, grandsire, e'en with all
            my heart
            Would[1] I were dead, so[2] you did live again.
            O Lord, I cannot speak to him for weeping;
            My tears will choke me if I ope[3] my mouth.

[1] *I wish*
[2] *if it meant that*
[3] *open*

Titus Andronicus ends on an uncertain note. Will Lucius, who was so eager to put Alarbus to death, usher in a time of peace, or is further violence on the horizon? With the death of Titus and his enemies, have Rome's internal conflicts been resolved? Has Titus helped to save Rome, or put her on the path to ruin?

"We expect the tragic hero to win through to regeneration or revelation, but Titus does not. The play opens with his impious sacrifice of Tamora's son followed by the unnatural slaying of his own son Mutius, and ends with his savage revenge against Tamora and her remaining sons followed by the slaying of his own daughter ... in Shakespeare's later tragedies, we are reconciled to the hero's death when we are shown how out of the strong came forth sweetness ... no such consolation comes at the end of Titus Andronicus.*"*

A. C. Hamilton, *Titus Andronicus: The Form of Shakespearean Tragedy*, 1963

The final victims

Like Titus himself, most of his adversaries – Saturninus, Tamora, and her two sons Demetrius and Chiron – are now dead. One implacable enemy remains alive, however: the empress's lover Aaron, held prisoner by Lucius and brought to Rome. Guards now drag him into the banqueting hall and bring him before the new emperor, who pronounces his verdict:

> *Roman Lord:* You sad Andronici, have done with[1] woes,
> Give sentence on this execrable wretch
> That hath been breeder[2] of these dire events.
> *Lucius:* Set him breast-deep in earth and famish[3] him;
> There let him stand and rave and cry for food.
> If anyone relieves or pities him,
> For the offence he dies; this is our doom.[4]

> [1] *leave, set aside*
> [2] *origin, creator*
> [3] *starve*
> [4] *my sentence*

Even in the face of a slow, agonising death, Aaron remains defiant. He scorns the idea of remorse, pity, or appeals to the heavens:

> *Aaron:* I am no baby, I, that with base prayers
> I should repent the evils I have done.
> Ten thousand worse than ever yet I did
> Would I perform if I might have my will.
> If one good deed in all my life I did,
> I do repent it from my very soul.

Lucius surveys the bodies strewn on the floor of the banqueting hall. He instructs his attendants to bury the emperor in his ancestral tomb, and to place Titus and Lavinia in the family vault, where so many of Titus's sons have already been laid to rest.

The emperor's wife, however, will not be given the dignity of a burial, and there will be no ceremony to mark her death. In a final act of revenge, Lucius decrees that Tamora's body, like that of a common criminal, will be left in the open to be devoured by wild animals:

Lucius: As for that ravenous tiger, Tamora,
No funeral rite, nor man in mourning weed,[1]
No mournful bell shall ring her burial,
But throw her forth to beasts and birds to prey:[2]
Her life was beastly and devoid of pity,
And being dead, let birds on her take pity.

[1] attendant in sombre clothing
[2] feed on, scavenge

The bodies are carried away in solemn procession.

———

Acknowledgements

The following publications have proved invaluable as sources of factual information and critical insight:

- Jonathan Bate, Introduction to the Arden Shakespeare edition of *Titus Andronicus*, Bloomsbury, 2018

- Judith Bock, *A Wilderness of Tigers*, Programme notes for the Colorado Shakespeare Festival production of *Titus Andronicus*, 1988

- Charles Boyce, *Shakespeare A to Z*, Roundtable Press, 1990

- Karin Brown, *Titus Andronicus in Performance*, in the RSC Shakespeare edition of *Titus Andronicus*, 2011

- Gale Edwards, Director's Notes for the Shakespeare Theatre Company production of *Titus Andronicus*, 2007

- Akiva Fox, *Dismembering Rome*, Programme notes for the Shakespeare Theatre Company production of *Titus Andronicus*, 2007

- A. C. Hamilton, *Titus Andronicus: The Form of Shakespearean Tragedy*, in *Shakespeare Quarterly* Vol. 14, Oxford University Press, 1963

- G. K. Hunter, *Shakespeare's Earliest Tragedies*, in *Shakespeare Survey* Vol. 27, Cambridge University Press, 1974

- Laurie Maguire and Emma Smith, 30 *Great Myths About Shakespeare*, Wiley-Blackwell, 2013

- Harry R. McCarthy, Introduction to the New Oxford Shakespeare edition of *Titus Andronicus*, Oxford University Press, 2025

- Gamini Salgado, *Eyewitnesses of Shakespeare: First Hand Accounts of Performances 1590 – 1890*, Sussex University Press, 1975

- James Shapiro, *1599: A Year in the Life of William Shakespeare*, Faber and Faber, 2005

- Albert H. Tricomi, *The Aesthetics of Mutilation*, in *Shakespeare Survey* Vol. 27, Cambridge University Press, 1974

- Bart Van Es, *Shakespeare in Company*, Oxford University Press, 2013

- Dr Susan Willis, *Shakespeare's Double Helix*, *Asides* magazine, Shakespeare Theatre Company, 2007

- Michael Wood, *In Search of Shakespeare*, BBC Books, 2005

Guides currently available in the *Shakespeare Handbooks* series are:

- **Antony & Cleopatra** (ISBN 978 1 899747 02 3)
- **As You Like It** (ISBN 978 1 899747 00 9)
- **The Comedy of Errors** (ISBN 978 1 899747 16 0)
- **Coriolanus** (ISBN 978 1 899747 21 4)
- **Cymbeline** (ISBN 978 1 899747 20 7)
- **Hamlet** (ISBN 978 1 899747 07 8)
- **Henry IV, Part 1** (ISBN 978 1 899747 05 4)
- **Henry IV, Part 2** (ISBN 978 1 899747 25 2)
- **Henry V** (ISBN 978 1 899747 26 9)
- **Julius Caesar** (ISBN 978 1 899747 11 5)
- **King Lear** (ISBN 978 1 899747 03 0)
- **Love's Labour's Lost** (ISBN 978 1 899747 23 8)
- **Macbeth** (ISBN 978 1 899747 04 7)
- **Measure for Measure** (ISBN 978 1 899747 14 6)
- **The Merchant of Venice** (ISBN 978 1 899747 13 9)
- **The Merry Wives of Windsor** (ISBN 978 1 899747 18 4)
- **A Midsummer Night's Dream** (ISBN 978 1 899747 09 2)
- **Much Ado About Nothing** (ISBN 978 1 899747 17 7)
- **Othello** (ISBN 978 1 899747 12 2)
- **Pericles** (ISBN 978 1 899747 24 5)
- **Richard II** (ISBN 978 1 899747 19 1)
- **Richard III** (ISBN 978 1 899747 22 1)
- **Romeo & Juliet** (ISBN 978 1 899747 10 8)
- **The Tempest** (ISBN 978 1 899747 08 5)
- **Titus Andronicus** (ISBN 978 1 899747 27 6)
- **Twelfth Night** (ISBN 978 1 899747 01 6)
- **The Winter's Tale** (ISBN 978 1 899747 15 3)

www.shakespeare-handbooks.com

www.ingramcontent.com/pod-product-compliance
Lightning Source LLC
Chambersburg PA
CBHW061752020426
42331CB00006B/1446